Making the most of Clematis

by Raymond J. Evison

Published 1979 by Floraprint Limited, Nottingham. Printed in England.
Reprinted 1985, 1986.

ISBN 0 903001 36 5 (paperback edition)

Raymond Evison began his interest in the genus *Clematis* at a very early age at Treasures of Tenbury Limited, when as a young boy at school he helped his father and John Treasure, who in those early years of a newly-formed company were collecting plants and exploring methods of production.

After several years of working under the firm guidance of his father and John Treasure he now holds the position of Managing Director, responsible for the annual production of more than a quarter of a million clematis plants. Perfection has always been his aim and the Gold Medal Awards received at the Royal Horticultural Society's Chelsea Show testify to this.

Raymond Evison's knowledge of clematis is based on years of practical experience and his love of plants must be obvious to those who have attended his lectures, both in this country and abroad.

Contents

Acknowledgements

The Author and Publisher wish to thank Michael Warren for his excellent photography and John Treasure for the use of his garden at Burford House, Tenbury Wells.

The *viticella* hybrids 'Abundance', 'Little Nell' and 'Minuet' clambering over winter flowering heathers.

An introduction to clematis

The extent of the range of clematis available today, differing size and colour of flowers, flowering period, the type of growth, variations in foliage etc., gives the gardener nearly too much scope in making a decision and selection of what species or cultivar to plant where and with what. But it allows the imaginative gardener and plantsman an unlimited freedom of choice of planting site, colour combination and plant association. Creating a colour scheme with foliage and flower as if an artist, not with a brush, but with living plants, not on a canvas but a garden; what could be more exciting or rewarding?

The genus clematis (yes, it is pronounced klem-a-tis) is a most rewarding and fascinating group of plants which varies enormously throughout the world in the shape and formation of its flowers, leaves and leaflets. Most of the species native of the northern hemisphere are deciduous with two exceptions, *cirrhosa* and its cutleaf form *cirrhosa balearica,* both coming from the Balearic Isles in the Mediterranean. The southern hemisphere greatly extends the variation with many unusual forms and the semi-hardy Australasian species add charm to the range we are able to grow with protection in the northern hemisphere.

The flowers of the species vary dramatically in form and shape, from the nodding, pitcher-shaped flowers of the American clematis, through to the small bell and star-shaped flowers of the European

C. texensis 'Gravetye Beauty' displaying its miniature tulip-like flowers on *Erica vagans* 'Lyonesse'.

2

clematis, to the large, flat, erectly-held flowers of the species which hail from the Far East. Not forgetting the important and great wealth of species which are native of the Himalayan mountain range, Nepal and Tibet.

This great variation of the species extends to the hybrid and large flowered clematis that have been produced during the last one hundred and twenty years and which are still amongst the most popular cultivars of modern gardens.

For the more technically minded there are over three hundred clematis species distributed throughout the world. This book will be concerned mainly with the species and their hybrids which are native of the northern hemisphere, their cultivation and uses in a modern garden, whether it be formal, informal, patio or the natural woodland garden, where the robust species can be allowed to run riot, enjoying life to the full with the freedom to ramble and climb without restriction.

Regrettably, many of the three hundred species have no, or at least little garden value, and are of interest only to the clematis collector, botanist or hybridist. However, their presence has given rise to the very splendid hybrids of today.

The clematis of important garden value that are offered for sale and grown in their millions today may be divided into three main groups. The splitting and grouping is used purely for the convenience of cultivation, for the ease of identifying the flowering habits and most of all the pruning requirements.

Group one consists of the charming species and their hybrids which produce their main batch of flowers before the middle of May. The flowers are produced on short flower stalks directly from the leaf axil bud,

The lantern-like flowers of *C. tangutica*, a rampant species from China.

C. 'Edith', a free flowering plant over a long season.

C. macropetala 'Markham's Pink', a delightful form of the spring flowering Himalayan species.

C. viticella 'Etoile Violette' in full glory during July and August.

generally on the previous season's ripened stems. This group has a range of species, including the evergreen forms, which flower during January, February and April, the delightful nodding *alpina* and *macropetala* types which flower in April and our old reliable friend *C. montana* and its relations which also fall into this group, although their rampaging nature is so unlike the more compact habit of the evergreen forms and the *alpinas*.

Group two also produce their flowers from stems which grew the previous year and became ripened before the autumn frosts. The ripened leaf axil buds produce strong new growths which vary in length from 8-30cm with a flower at each growing tip. This group consists of the early large flowered cultivars such as 'Nelly Moser' and 'The President'; the strange double and semi-doubles e.g. 'Vyvyan Pennell' and the very large flowered hybrids such as 'Marie Boisselot' which start flowering before the end of June.

Group three flower on new growth from July onwards, all the previous season's stems become almost useless and die away naturally each autumn. This group of clematis are most useful garden plants and vary from the large open flowers of the *jackmanii* types to the starry-shaped flowers of some of the European species to the dainty nodding flower of the yellow *C. orientalis* from Tibet. The interesting clematis of herbaceous habit also fit into this group varying in flower and foliage, from the delightful urn-shaped flowers of some of the North American species to the nodding European species of *integrifolia* and the hyacinth-like flowers of the *heracleifolia* types.

Flower colours
The selection of flower form and

The flowers of C. 'Perle d'Azur', both in colour and form, add charm to any garden.

flowering habit is indeed extensive and the variation in flower colour is quite fascinating. The delicate shades to choose from are mostly pastel colours, not overpowering or too loud, allowing freedom of colour association with other plants and flowers. Purple, blue and mauve are the predominant colours, although regrettably the blue is not a clear blue as with a delphinium which is a close relative of the clematis, both being members of the Ranunculaceae family. The reds also are not a pure colour since the nearest true red contains shades of blue or purple, but they blend perfectly with most garden planting schemes. The pinks are refreshing and are of various pastel shades, frequently having two tones, giving a bar or star-like appearance as with the ever popular 'Nelly Moser', whose blossoms are often described as

C. 'John Warren', a plant for a north facing position.

resembling small cart-wheels. Even the deepest shades of pink fade gently in bright sunlight and are therefore not ideal for a sunny, south facing position. This disadvantage can, however, be used to advantage because the early flowering pinks are ideal for brightening up a dull north facing position where the sun's rays do not reach the freshly opened flowers prematurely fading them. A large flowered, deep buttercup yellow clematis is yet to be produced and, for the time being, the yellows are represented by the nodding, small flowered clematis species. The white flowered clematis are very elegant and some of my favourite clematis are amongst the whites. Many of the large flowered hybrids have such a pure colouring and the starry-flowered species look superb if allowed to grow through dark foliaged evergreens, such as hollies and pines.

The strange double flowers of C. 'Duchess of Edinburgh' with green outer sepals.

The colourful part of a clematis flower is not called a petal as with most garden flowers but a sepal. The petals are absent, except in the case of some of the *alpina* and *macropetala* clematis which have petaloid stamens. Many garden flowers such as the rose have green sepals, and colourful petals, the sepals protecting and guarding the delicate petals as they form in the flower bud before the flower opens. During a season when plants are producing their flowers late due to bad weather conditions, some clematis flowers often open green, the correct colour appearing later as the flowers age and the sepals are subjected to the sun's rays. Often, if this occurs, the flowers do not completely attain the true colour, the centre of the sepal remaining slightly green. This is almost certain to occur with white, or very pale pink or pale blue coloured hybrids. The May flowering cultivars of the large

C. 'Ernest Markham', a free flowering 'red' for a south facing position.

The stunning double flowers of *C.* 'Beauty of Worcester' are produced during the early summer months.

flowered section (group two) should be planted where they will receive some direct sunlight. They should not be planted in a cold north facing position. The varieties susceptible to this unwanted greening of flowers are noted in the Glossary on pages 72 to 75 and are not recommended for a north facing position. These green flowers are delightful if one is a keen flower arranger, or has a taste for the unusual. My plant of 'Yellow Queen' growing on *Garrya elliptica*, which is on a cold north-east facing position, always produces her first flower in a delicate shade of creamy-green, which never fails to arouse interest with visitors to my home.

Scent

We are fortunate to have a small selection of clematis which give a pleasant scent; regrettably even with the wildest imagination and on the warmest spring evening this perfume cannot be compared with that of a rose. The species *flammula* which comes from Portugal is perhaps the clematis with the strongest scent, the fragrance reminds one of almonds. Another European species *recta*, a clematis of herbaceous habit, has a very sickly sweet scent which is so heavy it is nearly unpleasant. A delightful, pale pink *montana* variety called 'Elizabeth' has a most heavenly scent when in full flower at the end of April. On a warm evening one is sometimes tempted to linger in one's garden with the scent of 'Elizabeth' until the moon rises! A few of the large flowered clematis have a woody scent, that perhaps of violets, but one's imagination is most definitely needed with all of these, with the exception of 'Fair Rosamund'. Unfortunately her flowers are a washy pink or off-white, not the best of clematis from the point of view of flowering or long performance, but worthy of garden space, although not for scent alone.

The foliage of *C. heracleifolia* 'Davidiana' when it becomes dry during the early part of winter is very heavily scented and this is possibly the reason why the form was collected by the monk Abbé David such a long time ago.

Attachment of clematis to host plant

The genus clematis offers such a wide variety of flowering habit, size, shape and colour of bloom, even a selection of scented forms, that one wonders what other peculiarities can remain. As far as I am aware there is only one other, and that is the manner by which clematis attach themselves to their host. The clematis, unlike other natural climbers, does not attach itself by sucker pads such as a virginia creeper or the ivy with aerial roots. The clematis does not strangle its host, it gently twists its leaf stalk (petiole) around the nearest support, securing itself against anything except the strongest of gales. The gentle attachment of most species and cultivars is embarrassed only by the over-vigorous nature of the *montana* family, who if allowed to ramble up a wall on to a roof area are quite likely to gently, but forcibly, remove any tiles as they search for suitable supports, and light. The weight of growth when an established *montana* is in full foliage has also been responsible for bringing down telephone wires, so be warned, keep your *montana* family under control!

C. montana 'Elizabeth' adorning a one metre high fence alongside a pathway where the scent may be appreciated.

Choice of site and soil preparation

The position of where a clematis is to be planted in relationship to its host or support and the thorough preparation of the planting site are vitally important. Obviously, if the correct choice of clematis species or cultivar has been made, but it is planted without thought or soil preparation all will be lost, or at best life could be made extremely difficult for the unfortunate clematis. Plain commonsense and a little gardening knowledge are all that is necessary. I do not intend to give strict instructions, but describe some of the pitfalls, and advise on the most successful methods I have found regarding soil requirements.

A clematis will undoubtedly be expected to grace its host or support for many years to come, barring accidents of course, therefore, if even as much as one hour is spent preparing the planting site, that time is little in comparison to the many pleasurable years ahead to the reader who will religiously carry out the advice that I am about to give, if not insist upon. I must be honest regarding one clematis that now adorns a *Garrya elliptica* on my house. The *Garrya* is planted on a bone dry strip of soil on a cold east facing wall and through it grows a clematis 'Yellow Queen' most successfully. No thought or soil preparation took place, the clematis was simply placed under the shrub and inadvertently forgotten. When I finally remembered, the clematis had firmly rooted itself into the soil

C. alpina 'Ruby', a free flowering form of the very hardy European species.

through the thin paper pot it had been grown in. I apologised and gave the plant two gallons of water and it has never looked back and has flowered well every year since.

When considering the planting position it is wise to think and remember where the most successful clematis species grow in their wild habitat. The species produce many thousands of seeds annually, many germinate and start into life in various places, even in what appear to be bone dry cracks in a rock face. However, a dry summer and

then disaster strikes. The most successful seedlings establish themselves underneath the overhanging branches of a shrub or tree where their requirements will be satisfied. The host's branches will shade the clematis roots just below the soil surface at the same time allowing sufficient rainfall to penetrate to the root system and the clematis vines can attach themselves to the host plant. This simple lesson from nature of where the best clematis survive in the wild should be used as a guide line when planting in our modern gardens. No clematis

The many flowers of *C. viticella* 'Madame Julia Correvon' clambering through the pink flowering *Kolkwitzia amabilis*.

Planting a clematis against a wall

1 Wall, fence or post.

2 Top of plant's root ball at least 5 cm below soil level.

3 Soil level.

4 Base of plant at least 35 cm from base of wall.

5 45 cm

6 45 cm

7 Main base roots slightly loosened.

8 Garden compost or rotted manure.

9 Mixture of loam, peat and bonemeal.

10 Sides and base of hole broken up.

11 Small plant to shade clematis roots.

Planting a clematis against a tree

1 Strong cane leading shoots to tree trunk.

2 Additional support.

3 Soil level.

4 Top of plant's root ball at least 5 cm below soil level.

5 Mixture of loam, peat and bonemeal.

6 Sides and base of hole broken up.

7 Garden compost or rotted manure.

8 Main base roots slightly loosened.

9 45 cm

10 45 cm

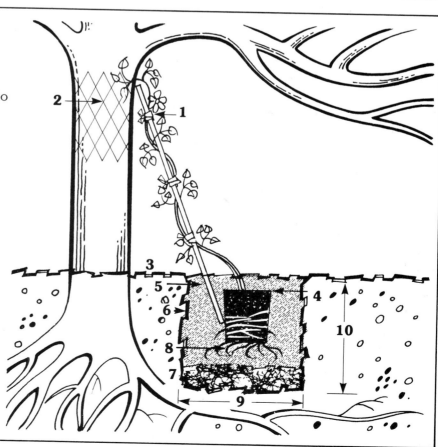

Planting a clematis against a shrub

1 Strong cane leading shoots to main framework of shrub.

2 Base of plant at least 60 cm from main stem of shrub.

3 Soil level.

4 Top of plant's root ball at least 5 cm below soil level.

5 45 cm

6 45 cm

7 Sides and base of hole broken up

8 Mixture of loam, peat and bonemeal.

9 Garden compost or rotted manure.

10 Main base roots slightly loosened.

in the wild would flourish or perhaps survive if planted within a few centimetres of the base of a wall in a bone dry strip of soil (unless the gardener has "green fingers" like mine!). It would be difficult for a clematis to establish itself at the base of a tree with a large trunk which would be surrounded with again very dry soil. It is possible to establish a strong growing clematis species in such a site, but it does take time, patience and lots of water. It would also be foolish to attempt to grow a clematis if its root system has to fight for every drop of moisture and natural food from the soil with the hungry feeder roots of a small tree or shrub. *Laburnums*, hawthorns and lilacs can be perfect hosts but their hungry root systems have to be overcome by the correct planting position, soil preparation and sufficient watering after planting.

It is advisable on all but the most perfect soils to carry out some soil preparation before planting. The exact site has been chosen, now the hard work begins. A hole to a

depth of 45cm with a diameter also no less than 45cm should be dug, removing the good topsoil and placing it in a different place to the subsoil from the base of the hole. The subsoil must be disposed of but the good topsoil can be used again when refilling the hole. Two bucketfuls of peat mixed with two handfuls of sterilized bonemeal may be mixed with the topsoil that has been retained and used to replace the soil that was removed. Before replacing the fresh soil the side and bottom of the hole must be broken up as it is vital that no firm flat surfaces are left surrounding the hole. If the soil is a very heavy clay soil, and soil preparation takes place during wet weather conditions, the sides of the hole will compact and appear to the young feeder clematis roots like an impenetrable concrete wall. If the base of the hole is not also broken up this may retain too much rainwater and the clematis roots will possibly spend part of each winter with very cold frozen roots, which may decay causing a

great deal of damage. Back to the important hole. Before it is refilled two forkfuls of well rotted farmyard manure, or well decayed garden compost, if available, may be placed at the bottom of the hole and lightly forked in; this rich compost or manure must be kept away from the young clematis roots and placed only at the bottom of the hole. The peat and bonemeal mixed with the retained topsoil may then be placed into the hole and lightly firmed using one's feet. If, when removing the soil from the planting site, the topsoil is found to be extremely poor then this can be replaced by using old John Innes potting soil, or a mixture of equal proportions of loam, peat, sand and grit. When planting on very heavy clay soil, or very porous sandy soil, additional peat may be used giving the newly planted clematis every chance of a quick and safe establishment in its new site. When refilling the hole, replace with a little extra soil to allow for sinkage.

Planting and initial training

When to plant

The best months of the year for planting clematis previously established in a container are the spring months, late March until the end of May or the autumn months, end of August until mid-November.

One must not rule out the remaining months. Clematis planted during mid-summer or mid-winter, will establish satisfactorily, but require much more attention. Nearly all clematis plants supplied by nurserymen are grown in containers and therefore can be planted throughout the year without causing distress to the plant, as long as sufficient water is applied to the freshly planted clematis during very dry weather conditions.

If a clematis is planted during the months of March, April and May the plant will establish itself easily during what is the natural period of growth for a clematis but it is important that the plant receives sufficient water until it becomes established. This may take five or six weeks before the feeder roots have become rooted into the compost provided in the planting site. Until this time moisture can only be gained from the root ball that existed before planting and water supplied by the gardener. As with other plants, do not just water the area where the stem emerges from the soil, water the surrounding area to a diameter of at least 30cm as this will then encourage the roots to grow into the surrounding soil looking for and finding moisture provided. When planting clematis during the months of June, July and August, it is vital for the plant's survival that it receives at least half a gallon of water per day during dry weather. The soil must be moist and stick to the fingers when touched. Check the soil 8cm from the surface. If only dusty soil remains on the fingers your clematis requires water, and this could be for a period of eight weeks until the root systems become established into their new surroundings.

If planting is carried out during the period between the last week of August, September, October and until mid-November, the safer and easier life becomes for establishment of your clematis. Unless the summer has been especially dry, the soil should be moist and the need for watering after planting will be limited. The soil will still hopefully be warm from the summer months and this will encourage quick root establishment. Clematis plants normally stop producing foliage from September onward until the next season but the root systems continue growing until the winter becomes cold and the soil temperatures drop low.

During mild winters when conditions allow the gardener to cultivate the soil clematis may also be planted. The plant will merely exist and not attempt to establish itself until the soil temperature rises and daylight hours increase. It is not advisable to plant evergreens, or the less vigorous species and cultivars during the winter months. Even species like *tangutica*, *montana* and *orientalis*, quite often will fail if they have to exist for several months immediately after planting in very cold wet soils, particularly if the soil is naturally a heavy clay and this can happen even when thorough soil preparation has previously been carried out. However, planting under trees where the soil is drier during these winter months can be an advantage. The soil condition under trees during this period is generally not too wet and can be warmer than an open garden situation, so that the clematis can start into growth as soon as the temperature rises. Hopefully the plant can then be partly on its way towards establishment before the dry spring and summer months when lots of water will be required to make the plant's life bearable until its roots are firmly growing into the new site. Under some overhanging evergreen trees this establishment could take eighteen months but be patient because it is worth the extra effort, and the reward will be yours when the clematis is in full flower.

Choice of plant

When purchasing a clematis from a nurseryman, or garden centre, it is not important that the plant should be the tallest, or the most costly. If the plant is in a pot no smaller than 7-8cm and growing on a 30cm cane and is strong in appearance with healthy foliage and a thick stem at the base of the plant, then this type of plant will grow satisfactorily. The smaller plant will take a little longer to gain maturity since one buys time when planting a larger plant. For successful establishment it does not matter whether or not the plant is in flower when bought. If the clematis is purchased during the late summer months, or early autumn, the leaves may be starting to die off, because, remember, most clematis are deciduous. If a clematis is bought during January, February and March, old leaves may still be left on the plant and to all appearances the plant may look dead. To check this the leaf axil buds should be visible by this time and will give a guide line to the plant's health and possible performance during the following summer. The choice of plant should be the plant that has several strong swelling leaf axil buds at the base of the stem (not at the top). With the late flowering species and cultivars, especially the *jackmanii* group, the new growth will appear right at the base of the previous season's growth, or even from below the soil level in the container.

Planting a young clematis

Before removing the plant from its container submerge it in a bucket of water for ten minutes; this will soak the root system thoroughly and will help the plant until the roots start to take up moisture from the freshly prepared site.

With a trowel dig a hole in the soil large enough to take the root ball, allow the hole to be dug deeply enough so that the root ball will be buried at least 5cm below soil level. This deeper planting will help in the event of damage during future cultivation, or by animals. If damage at soil level should occur in the future the plant will produce new growth from below the soil level, from dormant leaf axil buds. Therefore, in the event that the clematis stem should become severed, even on a mature plant, the plant would not be lost.

The plant may be removed from its container after the root system has been soaked but do not submerge for longer than ten minutes; plants, like humans, can have too much water! The bootlace-like roots of the large flowered cultivars which were at the base of the container and probably growing in ringlets may be slightly loosened but do not disturb the main root ball as this would be fatal. However, if only a few roots are freed this will help the plant establish much easier. On no account should the root systems of the fibrous rooted species and their varieties be disturbed and great care must be

Early March pruning and training of a Group two clematis showing a good framework of well-budded, lower stems.

taken with the root system when planting this type of clematis. The root systems of species such as *tangutica*, *orientalis*, the *alpina* types, *macropetala*, *fargesii* var. *souliei*, *flammula*, *serratifolia* and *vitalba* are all quite distinctive from the large flowered cultivars. They all have very fine, thread-like root systems when young plants, as compared to the thick bootlace-type of roots of the large flowered cultivars. If in doubt don't disturb the root system.

The plant can be placed gently into the hole and firmed well by pressing the soil carefully, but firmly, around the root ball.

Initial training

The cane or support which the clematis stem has been attached to in the container must not be removed. Another cane should be placed near the root ball, secured to the existing one and then itself secured to the host plant or support. The main stem of the clematis must have a firm support, otherwise unnecessary damage may occur through wind. As the newly planted clematis produces new growth this should be carefully trained and tied into position on the supporting cane until the stems reach the support or the main framework of the host plant or tree. As a firm rule all newly planted clematis should be pruned down to at least 30cm the first February-March after planting. This almost severe action will be rewarded by a more bushy, compact clematis. It is important that a strong framework of lower stems is established and the young clematis must not be allowed to grow away producing only one or two stems. Admittedly, it is more difficult to achieve a bushy plant of the late flowering, large flowered cultivars due to their natural habit of growing from only just above ground level each year. However, hard pruning and pinching out of the young stems of the early flowering clematis is rewarded in a bushy, compact plant, well furnished with flowers. Give up a few flowers the first year and hope to get double or treble the following years. Be an optimist, as I am with my clematis and look to the future.

Moving an established plant

The replanting of an established garden clematis is always a challenge but with care and a bit of luck it may be achieved. The only time when success can reasonably be expected is during the months of late January and February when the plant is in its dormant period, or at least just coming out of dormancy. If the correct pruning procedure has been carried out during the plant's lifetime, a large proportion of the top growth must be removed, ideally down to about 40-60cm. The stems must be cut just above a pair of strong leaf axil buds, do not cut into an old stem that shows no sign of life. Tie the remaining stems to a strong bamboo cane which should be placed firmly near the root crown but beware of new shoots which

may be just under the surface of the soil as you will need every leaf axil bud and possible new growth points in the coming months. Dig a circle around the root crown to spade depth and a diameter of 60cm with the root crown in the centre. Carefully lift the root ball out of the hole, with help from another person; do not be tempted to pull the root ball by the top growth, that would be fatal. The root ball should be placed on to a sack or polythene sheet, taking care to leave as much soil around the clematis root system as possible. The clematis may then be replanted into its new site, which should be prepared in the same manner as for the young clematis, but of course a larger hole needs to be prepared. The plant should be planted at the same depth as it was in its previous position. The first spring and summer after planting the soil surrounding the plant must be kept moist at all times — plenty of water. The remaining top growth should be carefully tied into the support at its new site.

The large flowered hybrids are the safest plants to re-establish, the fibrous rooted species are most difficult as their very fine roots drop away as they are being moved and with very little root being retained re-establishment is generally not possible.

Annual feeding and mulching of established plants

For an established clematis which did not receive the ideal soil preparation additional feed or enrichment of the soil is needed to prevent a slow decline of the plant. The ideal time for feeding clematis is during the months of March, April, May and June when the plant needs every bit of food and moisture it can obtain to produce strong healthy foliage and flowers.

Feeding can take various forms.

If available, well rotted farmyard manure makes an ideal feeding mulch because not only does the mulch feed the clematis but, if spread thickly enough on the soil above the root system, it will give additional shade to the roots and also enrich the topsoil in the process as the manure decays. The mulch should be placed on the soil near to the main stem of the plant to a depth of 8cm and to a diameter of 50cm. Care must be taken not to place any of the rotted farmyard manure on the main stem, or foliage of the plant as this will cause damage. A space of at least 12cm around the stem must be left. If rotted farmyard manure is not available, a mulch of peat placed in a similar manner will suffice. The peat should be mixed with sterilized bonemeal at the rate of two handfuls of bonemeal per two gallon bucket of peat. After the peat has been placed on the soil surface it may be lightly forked in using a small hand fork. Care must be taken not to damage the feeder roots which will be very near to the soil surface. In the event of no rain within two weeks, the peat should be moistened with at least two gallons of water which will stop the peat from blowing away and will also assist the bonemeal to enter the topsoil and reach the clematis feeder roots.

If mulching is not a practicality, the use of a liquid feed is another alternative. There are numerous liquid feeds available and any of the well-known, brand named products can be relied upon. It is important, however, that the liquid feed chosen is a well-balanced general feed. The liquid feed can be applied during watering from April until the end of July as per the instructions on the container. If the soil where the clematis is growing is dust dry, the plant must receive at least two gallons of clear water before the liquid feed is applied.

Clematis in containers

Unfortunately not all gardeners are able to cultivate and grow clematis in the natural manner with the root system established into good garden soil and the plant able to grow through a suitable host plant. The exciting fact is that some clematis can be grown successfully in a container. Frustrated gardeners who are limited in the garden space they have available to cultivate plants, people with only small patio gardens, or even those who have to put up with the ever-increasing spread of concrete, can take advantage of growing clematis in this way. Container grown clematis open up many possibilities for brightening up dull parts of a concrete yard area, along the walls of buildings that are surrounded by hard stone, or concrete pathways where no natural soil or flower beds can be prepared for planting. Naturally the conservatory, cold glass-house, or even a naturally well-lit living room or garden room lend themselves to the cultivation of certain varieties of clematis for pot or container culture. A 30cm diameter container with an early, large flowered clematis in full flower with perhaps twenty or thirty blooms will make an everlasting impression on any gardener's mind, and tempt even the anti-clematis person into attempting to repeat such a spectacle.

The correct choice of clematis is the most important factor but the correct size and type of container and the right mixture of compost are also vital. Other details such as watering, feeding, training and the general health of the container grown clematis need

A container grown clematis flowering during the late summer months, a valuable addition to any patio or paved area.

careful attention. Such detail and patience is rewarded each spring when the clematis starts into new growth which is followed by those handsome, large, colourful flowers.

The choice of clematis species or cultivar is, I feel, the most important decision to be made. However, this problem is made easier by the fact that the only choice is between those varieties within the early flowering group. If a container grown clematis is required for a small patio, sun lounge, garden room or balcony

16

C. 'Miss Bateman', a May-June flowering compact plant, ideal for container culture.

area, the plant should be of naturally compact, bushy habit which produces its flowers on the old wood, or the previous season's ripened stems. The *alpina* and *macropetala* varieties, the evergreen types, with the exception of *armandii*, are delightful "pot clematis", but the period of flower is limited. If area and space is not a problem and several different plants may be grown to flower over an extended period, then the small flowered types should be tried. If space is limited and only one or two plants can be grown, then one should rely on the early large flowered cultivars. Within this range there is a great choice, in colour, formation of flower and to some extent flowering period. Some of the first ones to flower in this group, 'Miss Bateman', 'Mrs. P. B. Truax', 'Sir Garnet Wolseley', 'Fair Rosamund' and 'Lady Londesborough' are very compact in their growth and flowering habit, but produce their flowers in one main flush during May and early June. They are ideal to train and make an absolutely glorious, if perhaps oversized, pot plant for a small area producing twenty to thirty flowers on a plant only one metre high in a container with a 26-30cm diameter.

The slightly later flowering types in this group are perhaps the most rewarding such as the varieties similar to 'Nelly Moser' and 'The President', which flower during late May and June and are also followed by a further crop of flowers during the late summer months.

C. 'Corona', a free flowering cultivar which makes a splendid container plant.

The most suitable clematis for container culture:

April flowering:
alpina 'Columbine'
alpina 'Pamela Jackman'
alpina 'Ruby'
alpina 'White Moth'
macropetala
macropetala 'Markhams Pink'

Early May flowering:
'Barbara Dibley'
'Bees Jubilee'
'Corona'
'Dawn'
'Fair Rosamund'
'H. F. Young'
'Horn of Plenty'
'Lady Londesborough'
'Miss Bateman'
'Mrs. P. B. Truax'
'Sir Garnet Wolseley'

End May-June flowering:
'Barbara Jackman'
'Beauty of Worcester'
'Bracebridge Star'
'Countess of Lovelace'
'Daniel Deronda'

'Edith'
'Elsa Spáth'
florida bicolor
'John Warren'
'Kathleen Wheeler'

'Lady Northcliffe'
'Lasurstern'
'Lincoln Star'
'Lord Nevill'
'Marie Boisselot'
'Mrs. Cholmondeley'
'Mrs. George Jackman'
'Mrs. N. Thompson'

'Nelly Moser'
'Niobe'
'Proteus'
'Richard Pennell'
'The President'
'Vyvyan Pennell'

July onwards flowering:
'Comtesse de Bouchaud'
'Madame Edouard André'
'Hagley Hybrid'
'Perle d'Azur'
'Jackmanii Superba'

viticella 'Abundance'
viticella 'Alba Luxurians'
viticella 'Etoile Violette'
viticella 'Madame Julia Correvon'
viticella 'Purpurea Plena Elegans'
viticella 'Royal Velours'
viticella 'Rubra'
viticella 'Venosa Violacea'

C. 'Horn of Plenty', a very large but also free flowering plant.

The *montana* group and most of the late flowering species such as *tangutica, orientalis* and *flammula* are unfortunately far too vigorous to be grown in a container successfully. Flowering of these types would be rewarding during the first few years when the compost in the container is fresh and contains the correct balance of foods, but when top growth reaches five to seven metres and the root system more or less fills the container, the gardener would be forever watering and feeding the plants. The late flowering, large flowered hybrids can be grown successfully although they do not make the same type of compact plant as the early large flowered group. The growth produced by this group, which includes the famous clematis *jackmanii* and its many forms, flowers on the new growth only, therefore, all the previous season's top growth is removed

C. 'Mrs. P. B. Truax', one of the most compact and free flowering clematis.

each February-March allowing new growth to be made. This new growth needs careful training and one should remember that the flowers are produced at the end of each stem generally after two and a half metres of growth has been accomplished. Despite the additional work involved, this group, plus the small flowered hybrids of the viticella group, are worth the extra effort of container growing.

The material from which the container is made is not important and the selection of a suitable container, whether of stone, wood, earthenware or even an old beer barrel must obviously be left to the individual. The size of the container is, however, important. It should be not less than 45cm deep with a diameter of 30-40cm, larger if available. There should be sufficient drainage holes. With a container of this size there should be at least three drainage holes each with a 5cm diameter, or five to six holes with a 2cm diameter.

Pebbles or broken pottery must be placed over the drainage holes to a depth of about 6cm; small stones and pea gravel scattered over the pebbles will also assist drainage and avoid the clogging of the holes with compost after watering, or by earth worms. Make sure that if the bottom surface of the container sits flat on the standing area that stones are placed underneath the container lifting it off the ground as this will greatly assist drainage and avoid blockage and water saturation of the container during prolonged rain or snow periods in the winter months.

In my experience, the only suitable compost to put into the container is that prepared under the John Innes formula, and John Innes potting soil No. 3 should be used. The No. 3 mixture is of extra strength, No. 1 and 2 being far too weak for long term pot culture. This compost is

This splendid clematis 'The President' flowers almost continuously from late May until September.

readily available from many garden centres and garden shops. There are many other composts offered for sale, including loam-free mixtures which contain a percentage of peat and grit or sand. They are most useful for short term growing of crops, especially annuals, but are of no use for long term pot culture where they require far too much attention to maintain a correct nutrient balance and where liquid feeding also becomes difficult if the compost dries out. When using John Innes potting compost the top 6-8cm of soil should be carefully replaced each spring using the same John Innes No. 3 potting compost. At this time, attention should also be paid to

the drainage holes, ensuring they are not blocked.

After the correct choice of clematis has been made, a suitable container prepared and filled to within 6cm of the rim, planting may now commence. Planting in a container is, or can be described as, re-potting and may be carried out at any time of the year, although obviously the points mentioned under the section dealing with garden planting should still be considered. Summer planted clematis will require more watering in order to achieve good and quick root establishment.

The plant, still in its original pot, should be plunged into a bucket of water and left to soak for at least ten minutes. Then carefully

C. 'Mrs. N. Thompson' produces a mass of flowers during late May and June.

remove the pot from the root ball, loosening the outer, bottom-most roots slightly, as previously described on page 14. Bury the root crown at least 6-8cm below the soil surface of the container as this will help the plant's survival rate if damage should occur at any stage in the plant's lifetime by animals, or when pruning or re-potting is being carried out.

Pruning and training of a pot or container grown clematis follows the same basic principles as for a free growing plant, but careful pruning and training are more important if the best looking container plant is to be produced. The first February or March after planting (depending on weather conditions) the clematis must be pruned hard with all stems previously produced being removed down to 24cm above soil level. This severe action is necessary to encourage several new stems to be produced at a low level, thus forming the basic framework of the plant for the future. The pruning cut should be made just above a strong leaf axil bud, or better still, a pair of buds. These buds will be visible during February and March. When new growth commences and three pairs of leaves or nodes have been formed the growing tip must then be removed. This will encourage the production of two or three new shoots from each stem, at the stage when the new growth is still soft and green and before the unapparent leaf axil buds have become at all woody. The new growth subsequently produced should be carefully trained and tied into position on to the various supports that have been provided (more about the choice of supports later). If possible, train the stems to grow almost horizontal in a circular manner around the support framework, commencing as low as you can. After the hard work in the spring no further pruning is required until the following year

C. 'Mrs. George Jackman', almost perfectly formed semi-double and single flowers on a compact plant.

and you may now allow your clematis the freedom of flowering. I assure you, if you have been strong-minded enough to carry out this pruning the first spring after planting, you will be justly rewarded. The many plants which I have prepared for our exhibits at recent Chelsea Flower Shows were all treated in this way.

The selection of a support or framework for the container grown clematis needs consideration. If the clematis is to be grown against a wall or through another host plant, then the support is already decided, but an auxiliary cane should be led from the container to the main support or strong branch of the host. For the free standing container plant there are many and varied metal and wooden supports for plants available on the market. Simple cane or stick supports may also be placed inside the container and tied together at the top, wigwam

fashion. Metal rods coated with a polythene or plastic film and bent into various hoops or pyramid shapes are all equally interesting and worthy of experiment.

Throughout the growing season from early April until mid-September container grown clematis will need regular attention such as the tying-in of new growth as it is produced. This will only take a few minutes each week, but it is essential. Watering is the most time consuming job with each 45cm clematis container requiring the equivalent of half a gallon per day during the dry spring and summer weather. A guide to water requirement can be tested by disturbing the compost a few centimetres below the surface. If it is moist or sticks to the finger the plant will not require water on that day but if the compost is like dust then water is required. Do not give the plant small amounts of water at a time since this will only keep the surface moist and the area where the roots are at the bottom of the container will remain dry. If watering is restricted this will reduce the top growth, which will in turn limit the amount of flowers produced. It is most important to remember that sufficient water is a must with the cultivars which are expected to carry a second batch of flowers during August. Basically, watering reaches a peak during mid-summer when water will be required each day, unless there has been rain. Less water will be needed as autumn approaches and stopped altogether by the middle of October, except for very occasional watering to stop the soil from becoming dust dry. Liquid fertilizer can be incorporated during watering but never apply to dry soil; water first and then use. If liquid feed is taken up by roots which have been starved of water, the root hairs will be damaged causing unwanted harm to your clematis. There are many liquid feeds offered on the market and any reliable, brand name product is suitable. A well-balanced feed with equal parts of Nitrogen and Potash is best for the growing season. Liquid feeding should be discontinued by the middle of August because the amount of new growth made from the end of August will be naturally reduced and it is important that growth should be hardened and ripened for the following season, especially with the early flowering cultivars which flower on the previous season's ripened stems.

When all foliage has died and possibly fallen to the ground during the winter and the fat leaf axil buds are visible during February and early March pruning and training can commence. All varieties which flower before the end of June belonging to Group one and two should be carefully pruned. The amount of pruning required must be judged by experience.

However, as a guide to the beginner, all dead and weak stems should be reduced to the point where strong, swollen leaf axil buds are present. The "fat" buds are the ones which will produce the first large flowers during May and June. The selected stems that remain after pruning should be tied into place and great care must be taken not to knock off any buds or crack any of the stems as they are being trained. The exact position in which the stems are tied must be left to the gardener and the individual framework that is being used. However, if the stems are tied in an almost horizontal position new growth will be produced and grow vertically, giving a good cover to the lower

The double May — June flowers of C. 'Countess of Lovelace'.

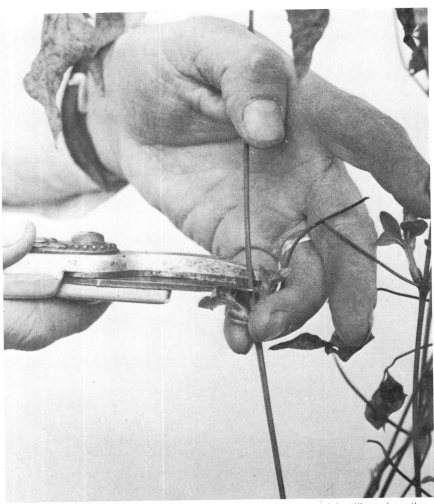

Pruning a Group two clematis showing the fat leaf axil buds which will produce the first early large flowers.

part of the supports. The stems of the large flowered cultivars should be spaced far enough from each other so that each swollen leaf axil bud will develop and hopefully produce a flower which will have sufficient space to grow without overcrowding. The decision of how many stems to leave, or remove, will be made easier by experience. It is easy to be greedy and leave too many stems which will cause reduced flower size.

If the later flowering types are being used, the pruning for this is the same as for the open ground or garden varieties of the same group; simply remove all top growth down to just above the swollen buds, which normally are in the vicinity of the base of the previous season's growth. As new growth appears this should be tied into position before it becomes over 30cm long. These stems also can be trained in a semi-horizontal position. If this growth is merely allowed to grow straight to the top of the support the plant will look less interesting and you will be disappointed with the result. The pruning and training sounds most complicated when written in this manner but do not be put off container grown clematis. Admittedly the work is time consuming, but it is most definitely worth the effort and time taken. The cold fingers experienced during the winter and early spring months, the backache etc., will be truly rewarded when the plants are in full flower, and the pain will be forgotten.

With experience gained over two or three years the enthusiastic gardener will soon start to experiment with different varieties to grow, or the shapes and style of framework used and many fine "pot plants" will be produced for the conservatory, garden room, patio or balcony.

If a conservatory or cold glasshouse is available, a

Tying the selected stems of a container grown clematis into an almost horizontal position, allowing space for all buds to develop fully.

succession of flowering "pot plants" may be produced by careful selection of varieties used and by the retarding and forcing of a range of plants. Varieties such as 'Miss Bateman', 'Fair Rosamund', 'Mrs. P. B. Truax', 'Sir Garnet Wolseley' and 'Lady Londesborough' which naturally flower from early May onwards can be placed into a cold glasshouse or conservatory and slowly be brought into flower by the end of April with the application of some heat. The slightly later flowerers such as 'Nelly Moser', 'Lasurstern', 'The President', 'Bees Jubilee', 'Niobe', 'Kathleen Wheeler' and 'John Warren' can also be used

for forcing or retarding. The retarding may be done by placing the plants on a north facing position out of direct spring sunshine. The *jackmanii* and *viticella* type also respond to forcing. The middle season flowering cultivars such as 'Marie Boisselot', 'W. E. Gladstone', 'Elsa Späth' and Ernest Markham' will continue flowering well into November in a cold glasshouse and although the flowers may be smaller and possibly not of true colours, they are still most delightful and give added colour at that time of year. Have fun and success and we well may meet at a Chelsea Show one year!

Pruning techniques

The pruning of clematis is probably the most talked about and written about aspect of clematis cultivation. What is a very basic and simple subject has regrettably been discussed and reviewed in such detail that the pruning of clematis has become unnecessarily complicated to the experienced gardener and newcomer to clematis growing alike.

Nurserymen in preparing their plant lists and catalogues, and I too have been guilty of this, have gone into great detail regarding pruning, listing species and cultivars under different types of clematis, generally relating to the former large flowered species from the Far East and the various other species that gave rise to the many hybrids produced. The problems and detail increased and became more entangled as new hybrids were produced and offered for sale. Therefore, with every good intention to help and assist their customers and readers, the nursery trade and writers of gardening periodicals have given rise to much unnecessary confusion regarding pruning.

As a gardener gains experience with growing clematis he will try to vary his pruning technique to suit an individual plant's own growth pattern which can change from year to year. Whatever he does, the gardener's aim will be to achieve the largest number of good quality flowers and healthy foliage.

After making the initial statement that pruning is a simple exercise, I have carried on to explain that pruning can then be varied from the basic technique as experience is gained, and it is at this point that confusion has occurred with conflicting opinions being offered to the gardener. My intention, therefore, is to give the reader basic pruning requirements from the first spring after planting for each of the three different groups of clematis which were described on page 3. If you subsequently want to find out which type of basic pruning your own clematis should receive, look up the name of the plant in the Glossary on pages 72 to 75 and there you will find the pruning group specified.

If you are a beginner to clematis growing the techniques illustrated below are entirely adequate and I suggest you delay reading my comments on more advanced pruning and training until you feel quite confident with the basic methods!

Basic pruning requirements of Group one (e.g. *C. montana*)

These clematis produce their flowers before the end of May on short flower stalks usually in clusters of two or more directly from a leaf axil bud.

1st February — March. Cut back all stems to 30 cm.

2nd February — March. Cut back all stems to 1 metre.

3rd and subsequent years. After flowering cut out any weak or dead stems.

KEY

▬▬▬	3rd year
▬▬▬	2nd year
▬▬▬	1st year

Basic pruning requirements of Group two (e.g. C. 'Nelly Moser')

These clematis produce their flowers on short stems which have grown directly from the previous season's ripened leaf axil buds. A single flower is borne on each stem; flowering commences before the end of June.

1st February — March. Cut back all stems to 30 cm.

2nd February — March. Cut back all stems to 1 metre.

3rd February — March and subsequent years. Cut back all stems to a strong pair of buds.

Basic pruning requirements of Group three (e.g. C. 'Jackmanii Superba')

These clematis produce all their flowers on current season's stems, several flowers to each stem, from July onwards.

1st February — March. Cut back all stems to 30 cm.

2nd February — March and subsequent years. Reduce all stems to just above the base of the previous season's growth within 75 cm of soil level.

For the more experienced gardener the following detail may be of further guidance. You will have gathered that clematis either flower on previous season's ripened stems, or on stems produced during the current flowering season. The date when the clematis starts to flower is the all-important point and with this in mind pruning requirements become self-explanatory as one either leaves the old stems on the plants to obtain early flowers, or removes the old spent growth from the previous season, making way for the new growth on which flowers will be borne.

Group one. The species and cultivars that fit into this group produce their flowers on short flower stalks directly from a leaf axil bud, generally on stems produced the previous season which became ripened by the early autumn. The clematis in this group consist of the evergreen species and their cultivated forms, the *alpina* and *macropetala* types and the *montana* group. This group produce their flowers directly from the old stems and, therefore, pruning must not be carried out until all flowering has been completed. Pruning for this group consists of removing all dead and weak stems immediately after flowering.

Established plants five metres high or more are not normally pruned, especially if they are growing in trees. All stems should be tied into position or attached to their host immediately after pruning. If any of the *montana* group have become untidy, or have out-grown their allotted space, then this too is the time for any thinning out or severe pruning that may be required, again remembering to firmly attach remaining stems to the host or support. After pruning, new growth will be produced which will become ripened during the late summer and produce its

28

Flower development on a Group one clematis (e.g. *C. montana*)

(1) Flowers appear on short flower stalks directly from a leaf axil bud, generally on stems ripened the previous season.

(2) After flowering new growth is naturally produced which, in turn, will ripen before winter.

(3) Flowers will appear from these buds in the following season.

main crop of flowers the following spring.

Group two. Clematis in this group produce their flowers on the old or previous season's stems and consist of the early, large flowered hybrids, the double and semi-double and mid-season, large flowered hybrids.

The flowers are borne on single stems which vary from 10cm to 90cm in length. Whether the stems that produce the flowers are short or long, the first flowers are always produced from the previous season's ripened stems. The observant gardener will notice the swelling leaf axil buds from January onwards, which by the middle of February will have become fat and ready to burst into leaf. These are the buds that grow during the early spring months and produce the first crop of flowers from the beginning of May until the end of June. To the experienced gardener the

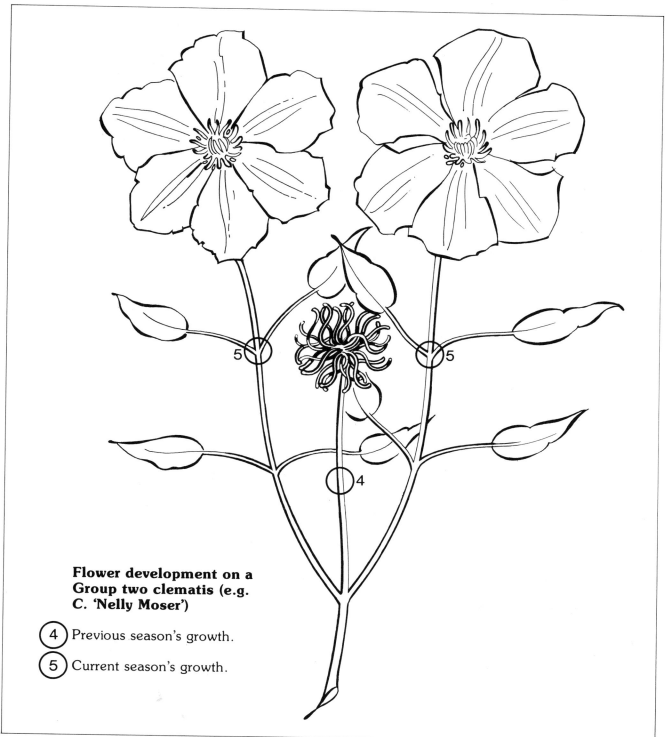

Flower development on a Group two clematis (e.g. C. 'Nelly Moser')

(4) Previous season's growth.

(5) Current season's growth.

clematis plant will be pointing out where pruning is needed and that is just above where these strong buds are visible. Therefore, the pruning requirements of this group consist of removing all dead and weak stems, shortening the remainder by 15-25cm to where a strong pair of leaf axil buds are apparent. All old leaf stalks that still remain should be removed, all stems that remain should then be tied into position immediately after pruning. The position for tying-in the stems is important and each stem should be given sufficient space where all anticipated new growth and flowers can expand to the full without overcrowding, or too much overlapping of growth. When the clematis stems are being tied on to a host plant be careful not to tie too tightly, this will only cause damage to the clematis and its host in later months, or years if metal ties are used. The pruning and tying-in of stems should be carried out during late February or early March when weather permits. It is best not to prune during frosty weather both from the point of view of one's fingers and the health of the clematis.

Group three. The third group contains the section of clematis which produce their flowers on new stems each year and in most cases each stem produces several flowers. The previous season's top growth becomes useless and dies away naturally each winter (unless the winter is a very mild one with little or no frost occurring when the growth may remain partially alive), therefore, all previous season's top growth must be removed to allow the current season's stems room to grow to maturity. This clean-cut, tidy up of the plant also removes any stems which may have become infected with mildew, or any other disease during the autumn thereby giving the plant a fresh start each year. The time for pruning is again late February or early March depending on weather conditions. The actual pruning consists of removing all old top growth down to where the strong, new, leaf axil buds appear, at a point just above the base of the previous season's stems, approximately within 75cm of soil level. The previous season's stems are identified by their mid-brown colouring, the older stems will be a much paler, light brown-grey colour. Many clematis within this group produce new stems from below the soil level each spring and this should be and is encouraged by hard pruning.

The clematis which are included within this group contain the *jackmanii* types and late flowering, large flowered hybrids, the *viticella* group, the *texensis* group and other late flowering species, including the herbaceous types.

An impatient gardener is sometimes tempted during a very mild winter to prune this type of clematis soon after Christmas. In my experience, do not be tempted because the strong, fat leaf axil bud may be encouraged to start into growth after pruning only to be severely damaged by a sudden change in the weather. In most cases if damage does occur to these buds the flowers are malformed and useless, so be patient unless your climate is a mild one. He who hesitates in this case is not lost, but is wise!

Established clematis which have not received the correct pruning needed for their particular type during cultivation and have become untidy, or bare at the base, are regrettably apparent in large numbers. After reading the pruning recommendations here one must not take a pair of secateurs to a late flowering (Group three type) and cut it down to within 75cm of soil level as this would, in most cases, be fatal. Due to incorrect pruning such a plant would most probably not have any active leaf axil buds within 75cm of soil level. My advice for such a plant is to remove all dead and weak stems to where active leaf axil buds appear, at whatever height this may be. As new growth is produced, this may be trained downwards to give annual cover to the bare, lower parts of the clematis. This will most probably be an annual job to attain an attractive plant.

The pruning requirement for clematis grown as container plants, or as ground cover, or over heathers and other special planting schemes should be checked under those individual headings.

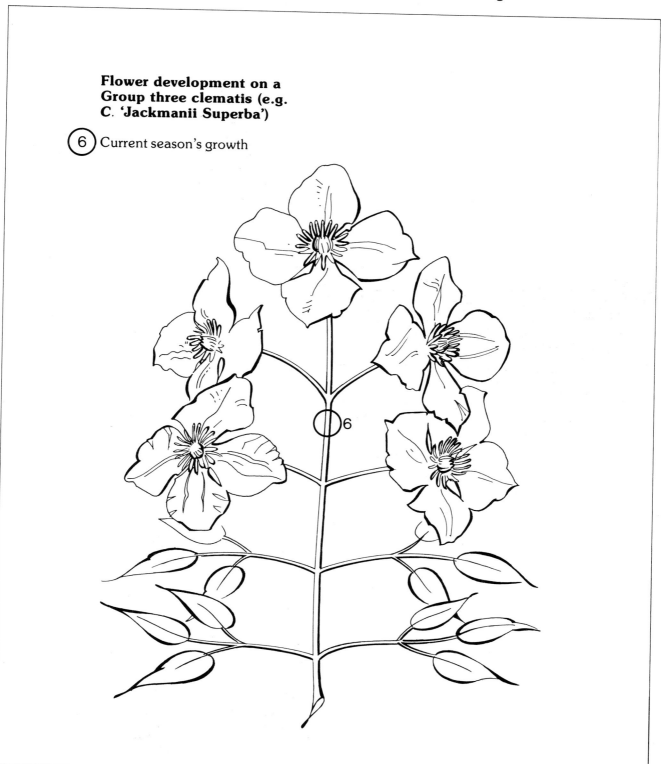

Flower development on a Group three clematis (e.g. C. 'Jackmanii Superba')

6 Current season's growth

Clematis as cut flowers

The use of garden flowers and foliage for flower arranging is becoming more and more popular mainly due to the high cost of flowers purchased from the florist shop. Clematis, both flowers, and foliage to a lesser extent, may be used to enhance arrangements. The foliage of *Clematis armandii*, an evergreen clematis from China is most handsome, the large, linear-shaped leaflets have a most unusual, strong, leather-green character. If stems of one metre are picked they are useful for pedestal arrangements when the arranger is in need of a strand of something to hang downwards. The evergreen foliage of *cirrhosa* and *cirrhosa balearica* can be also used for this same purpose. The fern-leafed clematis, as this Mediterranean species is sometimes called, is most delicate, especially the very fine, cut-leafed form *C. cirrhosa balearica*.

When selecting a clematis flower from the garden for picking one should choose a flower which has a thick, strong stem, not one which will bend when picked, otherwise, due to the structure of a weak stem, the flower may collapse within hours of picking. Choose a flower with a strong stem, a flower that has just opened or if possible one that is three-quarters of the way open at the point when the sepals are about to expand to their full size. When an open flower is picked beware of the condition of the centre of the flower; the stamens should be still held together and not have started to unfold toward the base of the sepals. After selecting the perfect young flower

The use of clematis flowers in a mixed foliage arrangement.

and the stem has been cut from the plant, the length is not important, the foliage should be removed to reduce transpiration from the leaves. The stem should be placed immediately into cold water as deeply as possible and the flowers can then be conditioned in cold water, if possible overnight. Depending upon the situation of the flower

arrangement and the room condition, clematis flowers that I have used have been known to last for ten days, however, four to five days is the average time.

In recent years while my company has exhibited at the famous Chelsea Flower Show I have used cut clematis flowers and some have lasted the full five days of the Show which is indeed remarkable in the heat and conditions of an exhibit under canvas. While using cut flowers in this way I have grown plants especially in beds in a cold glasshouse using a little heat to bring the flowers on, to open at the correct time. If the reader is fortunate enough to have the space available in a conservatory or cold glasshouse, growing clematis in this way for cut flowers is most rewarding. When clematis are grown in soil beds under glasshouse conditions, long high temperture periods should be avoided; the best clematis flowers for picking are those which have been grown under almost outdoor conditions, but with protection from wind and rain. Clematis grown in this way will naturally be several weeks ahead of outdoor plants. Hard pruning of all clematis grown especially for cut flowers is important as strong new growth needs to be encouraged and even established, early large flowered hybrids should be pruned down to about one metre each February.

After many of the clematis flowers have died away they are often replaced by delightful fluffy seed heads. If the old flower head and flower stalks remain and are not trimmed off, within several weeks the pollinated seeds begin to grow. As the seed tails (styles) mature and become a silvery-grey colour they add yet another attractive dimension to the clematis plant. As the seed heads become of interest to the flower arranger they may be cut for immediate use or dried to preserve them for dried winter arrangements. If you are particularly interested in growing clematis with attractive seed heads then the early flowering types are some of the best: *alpina* and *macropetala*, the early large flowered cultivars, *orientalis*, *tangutica*, *serratifolia*, *fargesii* and *vitalba*.

The most successful clematis cultivars for use as cut flowers:

Blue (dark)
'Beauty of Worcester'
'Kathleen Wheeler'
'Lasurstern'
'Lord Nevill'
'Richard Pennell'
'Serenata'
'The President'

Mauve
'Barbara Jackman'
'Horn of Plenty'
'King Edward VII'
'Vyvyan Pennell'

Blue (pale)
'Beauty of Richmond'
'H. F. Young'
'Lady Caroline Nevill'
'W. E. Gladstone'
'Wm. Kennett'

Pink
'Fairy Queen'
'John Warren'
'Lincoln Star'
'Nelly Moser'

White (creamy shades)
'Edith'
'Henryi'
'Marie Boisselot'
'Miss Bateman'
'Mrs. George Jackman'
'Yellow Queen'

The autumn seed heads of clematis are always attractive to flower arrangers.

Growing clematis through trees and shrubs

The clematis suitable for growing over and through trees fortunately amount to quite a cross-section of types. The early and late flowering species which rampage to seven metres or more and their respective cultivated forms, allow us a good freedom of choice.

Evergreen trees
Most members of the pine family may be graced with the many strands and flowers of the *montana* forms. The *montanas* grow eventually up to ten metres or more and look superb when they are in full flower, appearing like a white or pink waterfall as their many vines come cascading down over the branches of the large Corsican pine, or similar sized host. The growing of clematis underneath trees is rather more difficult than in an open position due to the usual dry soil conditions. However, if soil preparation as described on page 12 is carried out and adequate water is provided until the clematis becomes established, the gardener will be duly rewarded in the following years. Don't forget that establishment may take two growing seasons and in some very dry positions even three years from planting. When planting under a large tree such as a pine, a site within 30cm of the tree trunk is the most suitable position. The newly

C. montana displaying its many hundreds of flowers whilst climbing high into a large thuya.

produced clematis stems can then be tied into position by the use of wires until they reach into the framework of the tree's branches and attach themselves by the use of their leaf stalks (or petioles). The strength of the clematis vines will not be sufficient to cause damage to the tree. The best *montana* forms are the type plant itself, *montana*, which produces white flowers during late April and May. If pink forms are required consider *montana rubens* soft pink, *montana* 'Elizabeth' pale pink which is also scented, *montana* 'Tetrarose' deep pink and *montana* 'Picton's Variety' which is also deep pink but slightly less vigorous only growing to about six metres. *Clematis chrysocoma* pale pink and *vedrariensis* 'Highdown' are both near relations to the *montana*, both slightly less vigorous growing to about six metres. The two latter clematis and *montana* 'Picton's Variety' are suitable for growing through evergreens such as a large thuya or lawson's cypress and its many ornamental forms, green, golden or even the various grey foliaged forms which offer a perfect background to the pink flowers of the clematis. When the *montana* types are being grown in large evergreens and the initial hard pruning has been carried out to encourage the plant to become bushy at its base, they can be then left unpruned. If any stems become unattached from the branches of the tree then obviously pruning and tying-in of the stems immediately after flowering is the ideal time. This will then give the plant time to make new growth so that the following year's crop of flowers is not unduly affected by pruning.

Evergreen hollies can be graced with the tumbling blossoms of the later flowering species and small flowered hybrids. *Clematis flammula*, a starry white flowered scented species from Portugal looks magnificent when in full flower, the stems appear to be clothed with flowers and show up well against the dark green foliage of a holly. Many of the other pale flowered clematis such as the white 'Huldine' with its freely produced 6cm diameter flowers also look well growing through an open-branched holly. The yellow variegated holly trees lend themselves also to show up the flowers of the colourful *viticella* cultivars. Among the attractive range of *viticella* clematis, 'Abundance' wine red,

'Rubra' deep red, 'Royal Velours' velvet purple, 'Etoile Violette' purple with prominent yellow centre, are some of the best for growing in association with the lighter coloured variegated hollies. Due to the form of a holly tree and the importance of its appearance during the winter months a late flowering species or cultivar should be used, so that the larger part of the spent clematis growth can be removed during December allowing the holly to look tidy during the winter months with the final pruning of the clematis being completed during late February.

C. montana 'Picton's Variety', a good deep pink form of *C. montana rubens*, ideal for a medium sized conifer.

Yew, especially the large open trees, not the carefully trimmed ones, also lend themselves to the rampaging species. *C. fargesii* var. *souliei* a fine white clematis with 3cm diameter flowers which are produced in abundance from early July onwards looks delightful when it has reached a height of six metres on a yew and is in full flower. The delicate, nodding white flowers of *viticella* 'Alba Luxurians' look splendid against the dark background of the old English yew. This clematis is slightly unusual due to each sepal having a green tip, the centre is a deep purple black and the flowers are also campanulate in shape. As one can imagine from the description it is a little out of the ordinary and well worth a position in a large garden. Due to the important appearance of the yew during the winter months, the lengthy stems of the late flowering clematis may be reduced in December with the final and correct pruning being carried out during late February. The *montana* family, I feel, should not be grown over yews, purely because of the untidiness of the old growth during the winter months and this is why I recommend the later flowering species and hybrids for appearance and ease of cultivation. As well as the white flowering species *fargesii* var. *souliei*, *viticella* 'Alba Luxurians' both previously mentioned, 'Huldine' and *flammula* are also white and lend themselves to be grown and flower against the dark foliage of a large yew. Our native clematis commonly known as "old man's beard", or "Traveller's Joy", *Clematis vitalba* also needs a dark background to display its many thousands of creamy white flowers. The masses of silky seed heads from which the common names have obviously derived look best when the stems, which grow to nine metres, can be allowed to clamber up a tree.

Clematis serratifolia, which is similar to the more commonly grown *Clematis orientalis*, also looks well on a dark background. This vigorous species from Korea grows to six metres in height and has pale yellow flowers which are nodding and composed of four sepals with a central tuft of deep purple red anthers. The flowers are produced from early August until the first autumn frosts. The hawthorn scented blossoms of *Clematis maximowicziana*, again white, need the framework of a large tree to display its flowers. The species which attains six metres of growth needs a hot sunny position to flower well in the British Isles. Until recently it had been named *Clematis paniculata* but this name was found to be incorrect, thus the tongue-twister of a name that it is known by. In the United States of America the plant is still incorrectly called *paniculata*. For the garden which contains only a moderate sized conifer, yew or similar type of evergreen tree some of the mid-season large flowered hybrids and the later flowering hybrids may be successfully used to add colour and a variation to the white flowered species that need at least a ten metre high tree. Of the mid-season flowering clematis the pale blues such as 'W. E. Gladstone', 'Mrs. Bush' and 'Mrs. Hope', the pale pink 'Fairy Queen' or the pale mauve of 'King Edward VII' and the large flowered whites 'Marie Boisselot', and 'Henryi' may be utilised. The pruning requirements of these large flowered cultivars, if grown in such a situation need to be changed and they can be pruned fairly hard each February-March which will encourage plenty of new growth. Some old stems to the height of one and a half to two metres should be left to produce the early flowers. The hard pruned stems will then produce flowers later, during the summer months. The late, large flowered cultivars such as 'Comtesse de Bouchaud' and 'Hagley Hybrid', both of which are pink-mauve and the semi-campanulate, pale blue flowers of 'Perle d'Azur' may also be used to add colour and interest to the dark background of a yew which will display their pale coloured flowers to best advantage.

The gardener unaccustomed to growing clematis through other plants, shrubs and trees may be slightly worried and concerned about damage to the host when pruning is to be carried out. As mentioned earlier, clematis stems attach themselves by the leaf stalk (petiole) but this attachment is slowly reduced when the winter months approach. After several frosts the foliage of the deciduous clematis starts to decay and falls from the plant, leaving the leaf stalk loosely attached to the host. By mid-December, when I recommend that the Group three types have their top growth reduced to leave the yew, conifers or other evergreen in a tidy state for the remaining winter months, the leaf stalks will come away from their support without causing damage. There is no need to use a pair of garden steps to reach the clematis top growth which may have reached a height of five metres or so. The severed stems may be gently, but firmly, tugged from the tree or shrub, causing virtually no damage, and then burnt. The final and correct pruning may then be carried out during late February or early March as weather conditions permit. This double type of pruning when the top growth is reduced to one and a half metres or so in December is, in fact, an advantage ensuring that a good selection of active leaf axil buds is available when final pruning is carried out in February or March, which will keep the plant bushy and well furnished at its base.

The midsummer flowering clematis 'Comtesse de Bouchaud' growing through a large viburnum.

Deciduous trees

Whereas the soft and hardwood evergreens lend themselves beautifully to hosting clematis, regrettably the deciduous hardwoods, such as the oak, elm, sycamore, planes, limes etc., do not, due to the nature of their structure and also, in my opinion, the appearance of these elegant and graceful trees would be spoilt with climbers of any type clambering about their branches.

However, deciduous trees the size and shape of the flowering cherry, *Sorbus*, lilac, *Laburnum*, *Robinia*, even old cherry, damson, pear or apple trees that have passed their best regarding fruiting, but are retained in the garden because of their character and shape, or due to the shade given during the summer month's, are ideal. Any one of these types of tree may be successfully used to host the stems of a clematis giving the necessary support and allowing the flowers to be shown to their best advantage. The erect growing *Prunus* 'Amanogawa' which grows in a slender column needs the addition of another plant to give it colour during the period when its flowers have passed their best. The pale pink flowers of 'Comtesse de Bouchaud' look refreshing as they trail from this *Prunus* at two metres high and further upwards as the season progresses. The late flowering species and late flowering, large flowered hybrids are the most successful for smallish, deciduous trees. The reason for this is again because I like a garden, however natural it may be, to appear under control during the winter months.

Therefore the late flowering clematis may be provisionally tied up during December with final pruning being carried out at the correct time in February-March as described under the Evergreen Tree section.

C. alpina 'Pamela Jackman' in full flower during late April gracing this medium sized deciduous tree.

The selection of species or cultivar must depend upon individual taste but choice of flower colour, foliage association and the actual tree being used should all be taken into account. However, there are several additional points that need to be considered. The first is that the host tree should be studied regarding the position of the clematis planting site because the clematis branches will naturally grow towards the sun on the lightest side of a small tree where they will then flower. Therefore on a small tree some training of stems during the early part of each summer is required, so that one can then select the flowering position, because if left to nature the vines will grow into the lightest area which may not be the most effective place. On a large tree where the total circumference is much greater the position of where the clematis will flower can be more easily pre-determined due to the fact that the stems will mostly grow and flower on the side they are planted. When considering the flowering position of a clematis it is important, therefore, to consider both the height and type of host tree and the height of the clematis. As a guide, the ultimate height of the late, large flowered hybrids varies between two and a half and four metres, the species vary from about four metres and the *viticella* hybrids grow to about three metres in height. The density and colour of foliage of the tree is another important factor. For instance, if the foliage is pale coloured as with *Pyrus salicifolia* 'Pendula' (the silver foliaged weeping pear) a purple clematis such as the free flowering *viticella* 'Etoile Violette' or the ever popular 'Jackmanii Superba' may be used, but if the foliage is very dark as with a pear or thickly branched apple tree one must choose a pale flowered clematis such as 'Comtesse de

C. montana firmly attached to its host, a rugged tree trunk, with the help of discreetly placed ties.

Bouchaud', 'Huldine' or the pale flowered *viticella* hybrids 'Minuet', 'Margot Koster', 'Little Nell' or 'Alba Luxurians'.

As a further guide line the following planting association using a medium sized deciduous tree and one of the late flowering large or small flowered cultivars may be considered. The autumn flowering cherry *Prunus subhirtella* 'Autumnalis Rosea' is an ideal, open-branched, lightly foliaged tree giving the correct support and framework, where one of the *viticella* hybrids such as 'Abundance', 'Madame Julia Correvon' or 'Rubra' can be

shown to great advantage. In this instance one is adding colour to the tree during a period from July to September but the main clematis top growth is removed before the cherry commences flowering. The golden foliage of *Robinia pseudoacacia* 'Frisia' is an absolute must to display the purple flowers of either *viticella* 'Etoile Violette' which produces masses of medium sized flowers or the large deep purple flowers of 'Gipsy Queen'; both of these clematis flower from July onwards. To enhance the dense foliage of a *Laburnum* one should choose a free flowering clematis such as the *viticella* cultivars 'Margot Koster' with pale rosy-red flowers or 'Minuet' with delightful white flowers veined throughout with mauve. The contrast of the purple flowers of 'Jackmanii Superba', or the carmine-red flowers of 'Ville de Lyon' will also give much-needed colour to a *Laburnum* tree from July until early September. *Sorbus cashmiriana* with its fern-like foliage is an ideal host for late flowering hybrids like 'Star of India', a very free flowering deep purple blue and the rosy purple flowers of 'Victoria'. The clematis add colour and interest to the *Sorbus* after its flowering time and before the glistening white berries appear in the autumn.

Large shrubs

Both evergreen and deciduous shrubs lend themselves to hosting clematis. The list of suitable hosts in this section could be nearly endless. I must, therefore, leave the final decisions of combination to the imaginative gardener, but again there are some guide lines that may assist with the choice of host and the selection of the correct type of clematis. The large flowered hybrid and tall growing species rhododendrons lend themselves perfectly to support the twining stems of a clematis. The mid-season, large flowered hybrids need such a host so that their natural, free growing, open framework of stems can spread themselves, distributing their very large open flowers widely over their support. This group of clematis produces flowers on the previous season and current season's stems and this must be remembered when the clematis is being trained during the growing season. Some of the best mid-season, large flowered cultivars which grow successfully with rhododendrons are the lavender-blue 'Beauty of Richmond', the pale pink 'Fairy Queen', the red 'Duchess of

Two clematis, 'Lasurstern' and 'Lady Northcliffe', in association with *Viburnum opulus* 'Sterile'.

Sutherland', the superb white 'Marie Boisselot', pale blues 'Prinz Hendrich' and 'W. E. Gladstone' and the violet purple 'Serenata'.

Medium sized shrubs

A selection of early, large flowered cultivars, double and semi-double hybrids may also be used to grow through rhododendrons or a similar type of shrub which is not more than five metres high and where the proposed host does not have an open framework of branches where wind can blow directly through the host causing distress to the clematis vines by detaching them from their support. Due to the flowering habit of this selection of clematis and the closeness of each flower to one another and the shortness of the stems, the host needs to be compact. The choice of hosts including the *Rhododendron*,

40

C. viticella 'Minuet' dropped over the purple foliaged shrub *Cotinus coggygria* 'Foliis Purpureis' and winter flowering heathers.

cotoneasters, (the large-leafed, densely branched types) large pyracanthas, escallonias, *Elaeagnus*, laurels, magnolias and other free standing deciduous shrubs including established Japanese maples, *Cercidiphyllum*, *Cercis*, *Cotinus* and *Cytisus battandieri* are all suitable hosts.

Of the early, large flowered clematis a selection of the following hybrids will give a good range of colours — 'Barbara Jackman', blue with petunia bars, 'Elsa Späth' mid-blue, 'John Warren' deep pink, 'Kathleen Wheeler' deep plummy-mauve, 'Lasurstern' clear blue, 'Lincoln Star' pink striped, 'Lord Nevill' deep blue, 'Mrs. Cholmondeley' pale blue, 'Nelly Moser' mauve-pink, 'Niobe' red, 'The President' purple-blue and 'William Kennett' pale blue.

Double and semi-double cultivars which may be used include 'Beauty of Worcester' deep blue, 'Proteus' mauve, 'Vyvyan Pennell' purple-mauve and the semi-doubles 'Lady Caroline Nevill' pale lavender and 'Mrs. George Jackman' white.

Mid-season cultivars include 'King Edward VII' puce violet, 'Marie Boisselot' white, 'Maureen' purple and 'Serenata' rich purple.

If desired, a selection of late flowering hybrids can also be used to give a longer and more varied flowering period through the season; varieties such as 'Ascotiensis' blue, 'Ernest Markham' red, 'Gipsy Queen' rich purple, 'Jackmanii Superba' purple-blue, 'Madame Edouard André' dusky-red, 'Perle d'Azur' pale blue and 'Ville de Lyon' carmine red. The *viticella* hybrids may also be added to the list of possible varieties to choose from giving a good variation of habit and flowering periods for the gardener with a large garden who is in need of a continuity of flowers from May until the end of September.

The very large free flowering *C*. 'Kathleen Wheeler'.

C. 'Rouge Cardinale', ideal for a very sunny south facing position.

42

The free flowering 'Mrs. Cholmondeley' looks delightful when grown through a purple or grey leafed shrub.

Plant associations that I have found most satisfying include the use of *Pyracantha rogersiana* 'Flava' whose bright green leaves are a pleasant background to the plummy-purple flowers of 'Kathleen Wheeler'. The purple foliage of *Acer palmatum* 'Atropurpureum' is a superb foil to the pink flowers of 'John Warren', or the pale-lavender flowers of 'Mrs. Cholmondeley'. *Cotinus* 'Foliis Purpureis' or *C.* 'Royal Purple' with their outstanding purple foliage display

C. 'Victoria' displaying its flowers through *Cytisus battandieri*.

the flowers of 'Nelly Moser' mauve-pink, 'Perle d'Azur' pale blue and the white flowers of 'Mrs. George Jackman' to great advantage. The choice of *Cytisus battandieri* and *Clematis* 'Victoria' is a delightful combination when the silver-grey leaves of the *Cytisus* are looking their best and the yellow pineapple-like flowers of the shrub and the rosy-purple flowers of the clematis are all performing at the same time. The velvety-red flowers of 'Niobe' are displayed most effectively against the background of the variegated *Aucuba* or the slightly more detailed variegation of the various forms of *Elaeagnus*. The association of *C.* 'Marie Boisselot' and the grey-green foliage of *Cotoneaster franchettii* also leaves little to be desired.

Shorter growing shrubs

Compact, more densely branched shrubs such as some varieties of pyracanthas, compact forms of cotoneasters, evergreen ceanothus, *Camellia, Aucuba,* which may be free standing or wall trained, are all satisfactory hosts for the early large flowered hybrids and the double hybrids which, due to the size and density of their flowers, require protection from the wind. The selection of clematis in this case needs thought; one must take into consideration the flowering time of the host, one must decide if the clematis should flower before, or with, or after the host has flowered; the colour of the flower, foliage of both host and clematis are all vitally important considerations.

A selection of clematis for compact, lower growing evergreen shrubs includes the early, large flowered hybrids flowering from May onwards, varieties such as: 'Barbara Dibley' petunia red, 'Bees Jubilee' pink mauve striped, 'Corona' purplish-pink, 'Dawn' pearly-white, 'Edith

C. 'Vyvyan Pennell', a must for any garden with its free flowering habit.

white with a prominent red centre, 'H. F. Young' Wedgwood blue, 'Horn of Plenty' mauve, 'Lady Londesborough' pale blue, 'Lady Northcliffe' clear blue, 'Miss Bateman' white, 'Mrs. N. Thompson' blue with red stripes, 'Mrs. P. B. Truax' periwinkle blue and 'Yellow Queen' creamy-yellow.

Double and semi-doubles which flower from early June onwards include 'Countess of Lovelace' pale blue, 'Duchess of Edinburgh' white, 'Vyvyan Pennell' purple mauve and the semi-double 'Daniel Deronda' purple blue.

A selection of some of the later flowering hybrids which flower from July onwards may also be used to give an added colour range and continuity of flowering. Some of the most satisfactory are: 'Ascotiensis' bright blue, 'Comtesse de Bouchaud' pink-mauve, 'Gipsy Queen' deep purple, 'Hagley Hybrid' rosy-pink, 'Madame Edouard André' dusky-red, 'Perle d'Azur azure',

'Victoria' rosy-purple and 'Ville de Lyon' carmine red. *Texensis* varieties 'Duchess of Albany' cherry-pink and 'Gravetye Beauty' ruby-red also extend the selection of shapes, sizes and also the colour range from which the discerning gardener can choose.

The low growing shrubs which do not attain a greater height than two metres force the clematis to display their flowers below this height. Thus one does not have to look upwards to the sky to view the flowers at close quarters as with some of the previous plant association recommendations. *Cotoneaster microphyllus* grown as a free standing shrub rarely attains more than just over a metre in height making an ideal host plant on which the *texensis* varieties 'Duchess of Albany' and 'Gravetye Beauty' can display their miniature tulip-like flowers which need to be looked directly into to gain the full pleasure from their unusual shape. The slightly grey foliage of *Cotoneaster*

C. viticella 'Purpurea Plena Elegans' trailing over *Hebe rakaiensis*.

buxifolius vellaeus is a splendid foil to enhance the pale pearly-white flowers of 'Dawn' which are produced from May until the end of June. Both cotoneasters have a low arching habit and dainty leaves which cluster around the stems, giving an interesting contrast in foliage shape and colour, as well as emphasising the obvious attraction of the clematis flowers. Plants of *Ceanothus* 'Autumnal Blue' are occasionally grown as a free standing shrub in mild localities and the glossy green, evergreen leaves plus the powder-blue flowers which appear from June to October offer the possibility of hosting several clematis varieties, all of which can either flower before the *Ceanothus* or with it. 'Mrs. N. Thompson' and 'Vyvyan Pennell' both May-June flowering will also produce their second crop of flowers while the *Ceanothus* is flowering. The semi-double 'Daniel Deronda' will produce its deep purple-blue flowers before and while the host is flowering. The mauve-pink flowers of 'Comtesse de Bouchaud' would be produced while that particular host is in flower, giving an even greater combination of colours.

The grey foliage of *Senecio greyi* presents itself beautifully to show off the contrasting colour of early flowering cultivars such as 'H. F. Young' Wedgwood blue, the white flowers of 'Duchess of Edinburgh', the rosy-mauve of 'Hagley Hybrid', or even the dusky-red flowers of 'Madame Edouard André'. And so the combinations and planting can go on, creating a picture in one's mind one year, planting the next and hopefully seeing the realisation the following year and for many years to come. With a little imagination and careful selections of both host and clematis and good cultivation, one can achieve most satisfactory results.

C. 'Marie Boisselot', one of the best white clematis for cut flowers, growing over a large cotoneaster.

Using clematis as ground cover

Only a few clematis are capable of complete ground cover, in the sense of the true meaning of the word which is "to cover and smother the ground". When clematis species are found growing in the wild they either scramble around at ground level and eventually locate a suitable support on to which they grow and then climb to possibly flop back down the support, or climb even higher. From this description one can assume that many of the clematis species are suitable for ground cover, if this term is used loosely. The smothering types which will sprawl around until a suitable support comes within reach are as follows. *Clematis cirrhosa* and *cirrhosa balearica* are both evergreen clematis and native of the Mediterranean regions, but regrettably neither are completely winter hardy and to be used as successful ground cover need an almost frost-free position. They both produce creamy-white nodding flowers which have purple blotches in the inside of each sepal. All of the *alpina* and *macropetala* group naturally scramble and smother at ground level. *Alpina* a charming European species, has given rise to several hybrids, all of which have single, four sepal, nodding flowers, with one exception. 'Columbine' pale blue, 'Pamela Jackman' deep blue, 'Ruby' purplish-pink, *sibirica* white and its natural semi-double form 'White Moth' and 'Frances Rivis' a

The non-clinging clematis x *durandii* trailing through *Tropaeolum polyphyllum*.

C. 'Nelly Moser' flowering in an east facing position and contrasting effectively with a variegated grass.

C. 'Jackmanii Superba' growing freely through *Fuchsia magellanica gracilis* 'Tricolor' and a grey foliaged bedding plant.

slightly larger, mid-blue cultivar are the best named varieties. *Macropetala* which is a native of the Himalayas with lavender blue semi-double flowers and the pink form 'Markham's Pink' all look delightful scrambling around at ground level, especially if there is a rock or some form of support to give the plant added height and another dimension. The *alpina* and *macropetala* types will give a cover of approximately three square metres.

Clematis montana and all of its family make a very dense ground cover giving a cover of approximately eight square metres after three years. The reader will recall that this rampaging species can vary from white to various shades of pink and can attain up to ten metres in a tree, therefore, give your *montana* plant sufficient space to develop and keep the plant trained after each season's flowers have faded. Of the late

flowering species which can give very good ground cover *serratifolia* pale yellow, *orientalis* and *tangutica* both deep yellow are all capable of growing each year to give a ground cover of approximately six square metres. *Clematis glauca* a plant similar to *orientalis* and *tangutica,* but with the advantage of having glaucous, finely cut foliage is a little more out of the ordinary. The medium sized, white flowers of 'Huldine' look refreshing

C. 'Elsa Späth' trailing and sprawling at soil level through dianthus and other perennials.

against its deep coloured foliage when allowed to scramble at ground level, and it is also capable of covering five to six square metres annually.

The small flowered hybrid *Clematis* x *jouiniana* and its early flowering form 'Praecox' are one of the best smothering clematis because their foliage is coarse and the leaves large which means they give total ground cover. This hybrid between *Clematis vitalba* ("old man's beard") and *Clematis heracleifolia davidiana* produces delightful, soft lavender hyacinth-like flowers from August onwards. Its range is only about three square metres but it is ideal for ground cover and to scramble over short tree stumps which are sometimes in need of camouflage. As one would imagine, *Clematis vitalba* makes a superb ground cover plant. This species like all the others in this section are shown to best advantage if allowed to scramble over some form of vertical support and if no natural support in the form of a rock or natural bank, or rise or fall in the ground level is available, then something should be added. Stout branches of a hardwood tree may be placed in the site, with one end placed into the soil to a depth of 50cm or so to give stability. The branch may be cut to a desired size, or shape, and then placed into the soil at an angle to give yet further interest.

From reading several old books on gardening I find that clematis, and in most cases the large flowered hybrids, were grown on such supports as I've just described. The mind boggles at the thought of seeing clematis grown in this way as permanent bedding plants in specially selected beds with the added interest of shaped tree branches to give the necessary height. The later, large flowered hybrids would be best I feel because the beds could then be tidied up each

The blue-green foliage of this low growing juniper makes an ideal foil for the flowers of C. 'Mrs. N. Thompson'.

The May-June flowers of C. 'Lincoln Star' in association with *Hypericum* 'Hidcote'.

51

A European herbaceous species *C. integrifolia* growing in a mixed border.

spring, when all the previous season's growth could be removed. Mid-season, large flowered hybrids could also be used in this type of scheme and the plants would not come to much harm if they received similar hard pruning to the late flowerers. Their presence would add variety in flower shape, flowering time and colour range.

Personally, I feel that a flower border given over entirely to clematis would be rather uninteresting during the winter months, and here the use of several different types of evergreen shrubs would be invaluable. The ones I have in mind are *Cistus* x *corbariensis* and x *cyprius* 'Silver Pink', *Corokia cotoneaster*, cotoneaster

varieties like *adpressus* and *buxifolius vellaeus*, any of the broom family as they can look splendid with clematis vines trailing through them, especially if there is a breeze — *Cytisus albus*, 'Burkwoodii', *nigricans*, x *praecox* and *purpureus*. Other plants to consider are the evergreen *Daphne retusa*, *Erica mediterranea* 'Superba' a tree

The August flowers of C. 'Barbara Dibley' trailing over *Lamium maculatum* 'Beacon Silver'.

53

heather and eucalyptus which are pollarded back each spring and kept as bushes. *Eucalyptus gunnii* makes a splendid winter foliage plant. Also try *Genista lydia* and the evergreen hardy hebes, especially the grey foliaged ones. At the front of such a proposed border the rock roses (*Helianthemum*) can be grown making a marvellous carpet for odd clematis vines to trail on. Senecios, lavenders and the evergreen *Prunus laurocerasus* 'Otto Luyken' could also be used. I feel this gives a sufficient range to choose from which would provide a variety of foliage form, shape of bush and colour of leaf and flower.

Some of the shrubs which I have recommended for the special clematis border planting idea can also be used as individual hosts for some less rampaging late flowered species and their hybrids. The fascinating flowers of the American urn or pitcher-shaped flowers of *viorna*, *pitcheri*, *texensis* and the gorgeous *texensis* hybrids 'Duchess of Albany' and 'Gravetye Beauty' both have delightful little flowers which give the impression of being miniature tulip flowers, the former having a soft pink flower and the latter bearing glowing red flowers. The flowers of the latter open slightly more than the flowers of 'Duchess of Albany'. *Durandii*, a large flowered non-clinging hybrid with deep indigo-blue flowers with a cream coloured centre needs the support of a low growing shrub where its vines can just flop and ramble about. The elegant double flowers of *viticella* 'Purpurea Plena Elegans' show up very well when grown over the rounded form of *Hebe rakaiensis* (*subalpina*) which has fresh, apple green foliage. A semi-herbaceous clematis x *aromatica* looks most interesting when it is allowed to scramble over a grey foliage

One of the most rewarding plant associations using *C. viticella* 'Abundance' and other *viticella* hybrids with winter flowering heathers.

shrub, dispersing its small starry purple flowers over its host. As you can see, the options available to the gardener with imagination and time to plan such planting schemes is vast, if not inexhaustible.

One of the most successful plant associations that I have become aware of is the use of the *viticella* hybrids to grow over winter flowering heathers. A large bed of winter flowering heathers is splendid from early January onwards until April but the flowers of the heathers then fade away, leaving a rather uninteresting carpet of fresh green until the next flowering season in December or January. With the use of the *viticella*

hybrids the green carpet can be transformed into a very pretty patchwork of colours from July until the early autumn months. Clematis *viticella* itself varies in the wild from differing shades of bluish-mauve to white. It was introduced in the 16th century and has since given rise to many splendid small flowered hybrids; the ones most worthy of garden value and for the purpose of planting over heather are as follows: 'Abundance', deep pinky-red, 'Alba Luxurians', a fascinating white form with sepals that reflex, most sepals having a green tip. 'Etoile Violette' which has 7cm diameter deep violet flowers with contrasting creamy anthers, 'Little Nell' with creamy-

C. 'Dawn'. To obtain the best colouring this cultivar should be grown out of direct sunlight.

white flowers with overtones of mauve, 'Madame Julia Correvon', with wine red flowers, a rather gappy flower, each sepal twisting and recurving at the tip. 'Margot Koster', another gappy-type flower, with deep mauve-pink flowers. 'Minuet' which produces an abundance of semi-nodding flowers which have a white background and mauve veins at the margins. 'Royal Velours' whose flowers are so deep in colour they need a light background of one of the golden foliage heathers to show the flowers to best effect. The flower is a full round shape and the sepals are a deep velvety purple. 'Rubra' with masses of deep wine-red flowers and lastly the delightful, veined flowers of 'Venosa Violacea' which are the largest of this group reaching about 7-8cm in diameter with the boat-shaped sepals veined throughout with purple on a white background which give the flower a very fascinating appearance.

The method for planting the *viticellas* amongst heathers is quite straightforward. The clematis need to be planted at approximately one and a half metres apart and it may be necessary for a heather plant to be removed on an established bed. Soil preparation as described on page 12 should be carried out unless the heather bed was well prepared before planting. If a heather bed, which has only been planted for a few months, is to be used, it is advisable to allow the heathers twelve to eighteen months to become established so that the clematis will not swamp the young heathers. The clematis, when grown over heathers in this manner, should be pruned back hard each November to allow the heathers to start their flowering at the correct time and also to prevent rain-soaked clematis leaves sagging on to the heathers

C. viticella 'Etoile Violette', probably the freest flowering of all the small flowered hybrids.

A superb use of form, foliage and flower using the *viticella* hybrids over winter flowering heathers and conifers.

causing harm to their foliage and possibly spoiling their flowers. The amount of clematis growth during the summer months is not sufficient to cause harm and the heathers will not become spoilt or smothered. Due to the earlier than normal pruning of the clematis new growth may appear early the next year if the winter is at all a mild one. If this is the case, and there are also mice present in the heather border, damage may occur, and the prevention method suggested under the Pest and Diseases section on page 71 should be carried out.

The *viticella* hybrids are equally successful when used to enhance the flowers of the summer flowering heathers and in addition to the *viticellas* the *texensis* hybrids and *durandii* may also be used to give many interesting flower and colour combinations.

Late, large flowered hybrids can also be used to scramble through and over many of the summer flowering, annual bedding plants. *Clematis* 'Jackmanii Superba' looks splendid planted with deep purple-red asters and the effect is even better if several other taller-growing plants such as woolly-leafed *Helichrysum petiolatum* or the grey-foliaged senecios are dot-planted amongst the asters. The range of bedding plants is vast and I suggest that anyone wishing to try out this particular idea should spend a little time during one summer planning such a border with annuals and the permanent planting of clematis and looking in other gardens for ideas of plant and colour associations.

A trailing stem of *C. viticella* 'Venosa Violacea' in flower, showing a good contrast with *Calluna vulgaris* 'Robert Chapman'.

On walls, fences and roses

The selection and choice of support for clematis that are to be grown against a wall either directly on to a support or through a host plant.

You will have gathered, by now, that I prefer plants to grow in a natural situation, as far as possible. The placing of a clematis plant to grow against a blank wall goes very much against my way of gardening. However, I accept the point that in some cases this may be necessary and must be done.

The large, double flowers of *C.* 'Proteus' at their best with the evergreen *Ceanothus* 'Cascade'.

One of the oldest clematis cultivars 'Henryi' growing through a large leafed variegated ivy against a wall.

C. macropetala growing up through *Cotoneaster horizontalis*, showing good use of foliage and flower.

If a clematis is to be grown against a wall there are a few important things to remember. Firstly the soil preparation should be good and the plant should be positioned at least 30cm away from the base of the wall. The plant should be pruned hard in its first two years to encourage it to produce a good low framework of branches and the stems may be trained in a horizontal manner and then allowed to grow upwards. This pruning and training early in the plant's life will provide a well-formed plant and avoid that all too familiar sight of one straight clematis stem and then a bird's nest collection of growth about two metres above ground level. Several factors will influence the choice of plant — the area which is to be covered, the ultimate height which the clematis may reach, and the flower colour in relation to the colour of the background, here avoiding pale flower colours on sunny, south walls. The shading of the clematis root system and lower part of the plant is a must on a dry, sunny, south or south-west facing wall. The use of low growing shrubs such as lavenders, helianthemums, hebes, heather etc., will give the necessary shade to the root systems. The selection of support must be given thought and there are numerous types of trellis, plastic covered wire in various shapes, sizes and colours available. The choice must be left to the gardener to select the one most in keeping with the wall or style of house and the total height and weight of the clematis foliage which the support will have to carry must also be taken into account. On outbuildings ordinary 7cm wide mesh chicken wire or sheep netting for the vigorous species is practical, but this would not be the case if the site were adjacent to an important door entrance.

C. montana rubens flowering during May against a contrasting background.

C. 'H. F. Young' growing through a wall trained *Cercis siliquastrum*.

C. 'Maureen' growing with *Ceanothus impressus* and trailing on to the small shrub *Convolvulus cneorum* which provides shade to the clematis roots.

The clematis vines need to be able to reach a support in one form or another every 8-10cm either horizontally or vertically and to bridge the gap between soil level and the first strong support, a cane should be firmly attached to the wall support and the first growths of the clematis tied to the cane.

The use of a wall trained shrub has many advantages because the framework of the host branches or stems allow the clematis to grow naturally and with very little training being necessary. Obviously the host requires to be tied against the wall but the elaborate trellis and wire supports are not needed as most wall trained shrubs can be tied to a masonry nail placed into the wall at the required spacings. Most host plants should be given two years to become established before a clematis is planted to grow through them. The choice of host almost seems endless but some of the most satisfactory are the evergreens including *Azara*,

C. 'Ville de Lyon' against a bare wall. How much better this clematis would have looked growing through an evergreen wall trained shrub.

The single flowers of *C.* 'Daniel Deronda' climbing through a wall trained robinia.

Camellia, Ceanothus, Garrya elliptica, Magnolia grandiflora and Pyracantha. Other deciduous shrubs such as jasmine, Wisteria, Buddleia, Chaenomeles, roses, Cotoneaster horizontalis, Cytisus battandieri, etc., also give sufficient support. The selection of host and clematis is an easy one and the possible combinations are extensive. The clematis can be chosen to flower at the same time, or before, or after its host. All of the less vigorous species and all of the large flowered hybrids whether early, mid or late season flowering may be used. The clematis that need the support provided by wall trained shrubs include the evergreen, early flowering species and their cultivars, the double and semi-double cultivars that produce the gigantic-sized flowers which dislike a windy position and need the protection of a wall site and some of the less vigorous species, for instance florida bicolor and florida 'Alba Plena'.

On a north facing wall the alpina and macropetala types look delightful when growing through Chaenomeles. 'Nelly Moser', 'Dawn', 'Bees Jubilee' and 'Lincoln Star' with their flowers in various shades of pink brighten up a north facing wall and look well when grown through camellias or pyracanthas. Climbing and wall trained roses give the clematis vines plenty of support to climb through their branching stems. Here, the choice of clematis and rose is important so that the pruning requirements of the rose and clematis will be basically the same. Life can be very difficult for the clematis stems and damage may be caused if the rose needs severe pruning annually and the clematis does not each year but this can be avoided with a little thought. The point made in the last sentence obviously applies to

A colourful tangled mass of C. montana rubens and an early flowering honeysuckle

all of the other wall shrubs used; also thought must be given to the ultimate height of clematis and host since to grow a montana or tangutica over a Ceanothus or Pyracantha would mean suffocation for the unfortunate host within four years.

Posts, pergolas, fences and archways

The thought of using a clematis to clothe an individual bare post hurts me about as much as putting a clematis to grow against a blank wall. If posts are in need of being furnished with a shrub, I believe that both from appearance's sake and for the plant's well-being a clematis grown in association with another

shrub, such as a pillar or climbing rose makes a far better proposition. If space is only available for a clematis some varieties are better than others. The late flowering, large flowered hybrids are best. 'Hagley Hybrid' which produces masses of pink flowers from July onwards and 'Madame Edouard André' with her dusky-red flowers, also from July onwards, may be used alone if desired to give a colourful display. If a more rampageous clematis is required the montana types or the late flowering species such as tangutica and orientalis with their yellow, lantern-like flowers may be used, but they will need more attention especially when they are in full flower and

C. montana 'Elizabeth' covering a wooden fence in a delightful cottage garden.

A rustic fence festooned with *C. montana* during early May.

of the plants (from the previous season's ripened stems). The supports and posts of the pergola will also need clothing and the *alpina*, *macropetala* and early, large flowered hybrids will fulfil this role, producing their flowers from April until the end of June. The mid season and late, large flowered hybrids will give us flowers from June onwards and also give us more height with growth reaching the top of the support posts at two and a half metres and then trailing along to the top to cascade back down again covered in flowers. Hopefully the large flowered hybrids will also give a second crop of flowers during August and September. The planning needs careful thought so that the archway or pergola does not become too heavily laden with foliage, causing structural damage; stout support posts and rigid cross bars on the top should be used.

The pruning requirements of both host and clematis must also be observed. If any of the early, large flowered clematis are used because of the choice of colour, they may be pruned hard, the early flowers would be less, but a crop of flowers would be produced on the new growth six weeks or so later than normal. The kinking and twisting of stems when handling, pruning, or training other shrubs on the framework should be avoided if at all possible as they may cause partial damage to the vine later in the year when the foliage and flowers need every bit of moisture and sap the stems can provide. The clematis of different varieties but similar flowering period may be grown together but it is advisable to choose plants with the same pruning requirements. Life becomes increasingly tedious if one attempts to disentangle the growth and stems of a *montana* and a late, large flowered hybrid from one another during

foliage. The stems will need tying-in to avoid damage during any strong winds or gales and the supporting post will need to be of a hardwood with the bottom sunk at least 65cm into the soil and also firmly anchored in a concrete base.

Rustic pergolas and archways add charm and character to any garden and offer yet another place where the enthusiastic clematis grower may cultivate and grow a range of clematis. A pergola or archway given over entirely to clematis is not to be desired, however, but if other climbers and shrubs are used in association with clematis then the effect is tremendous giving

colour, flower and foliage for most months of the year. Climbing and pillar roses, *Lonicera* (honeysuckle), *Wisteria*, *Akebia*, *Actinidia*, *Ampelopsis*, *Chaenomeles*, *Hedera* (ivy) *Jasminum*, *Parthenocissus* (virginia creeper) *Passiflora* and *Vitis* (the ornamental and fruiting vines) all give a great variation of flower, foliage and form which is complemented by the clematis. The *montana* family may be used on a large pergola or archway and the stems and foliage will eventually give a great deal of cover and shade on the top of the framework. The flowers will generally be near the growing tip

February. One's fingers become cold, one's temper is tested, one's eyes become rather crossed and the clematis stems become damaged. Be warned, unless you are even-tempered and have good eyesight!

The use of clematis to grow over fences made of chain link, wire, or wood is one of the coldest places to ask any self-respecting plant to grow through or over. Therefore, only the strong growing species or small flowered hybrid clematis can be considered. The height of the fence is not important since a clematis will climb until there is no further vertical support at which point its vines will fall back naturally on to where it has grown up from. So if the fence is one or even three metres in height other than the requirement to cover the fence the choice of clematis is left open between the strong growing types. The *alpina* and *macropetala*, the *montanas* and the *viticella* hybrids, coupled with the robust growing, late flowering species such as *tangutica*, *orientalis*, *serratifolia* and *fargesii* var. *souliei* will all tackle the job and succeed. A selection from these clematis will give a good continuity of flowers throughout the season. One point to remember — if the fence is only one metre high a *montana* or *tangutica* can each cover such a fence to the length of at least eight to nine metres after about three to four years. A selection of *alpina* types and the *viticella* hybrids would be best for a low, one metre high fence giving flower from April until September with the exception of a few weeks during June. The use of a *montana* cultivar on a low wall, possibly alongside a set of garden

A wooden archway almost disappearing under the prolific flowers of *C.* 'Jackmanii Superba'.

steps, in association with a variegated-leafed ivy (*Hedera*) will make a colourful addition to any garden.

Clematis in association with roses

The use of clematis with wall trained, pillar or climbing roses on pergolas or archways can be most effective, each offering its companion either support or colour when the other is not in flower, thus gaining maximum effect from a small area of one's garden. The association can also be carried through to the garden where roses are grown as free standing shrubs. Every year the use of roses as shrubs is increasing. The old fashioned shrub roses include the splendid Gallicas, Albas, Damasks, Centifolia and Moss roses, all of which are easily placed in a modern garden either in groups, hedges or as specimen plants. The hybrid teas and to a slightly lesser extent the floribunda roses are more difficult to place in a garden if one wants to get away from the typical way of planting roses like soldiers in rows. The delightful "old roses" give us colour, form and scent, but regrettably have a limited flowering period as compared to the floribundas although their framework of branches and foliage give us the ideal support for the large flowered clematis. Due to the pruning requirement of the roses the late, large flowered hybrids are the best, thus avoiding the conflict of clematis stems to remain and rose stem to be removed. The gardener who knows his old roses may well use some of the early, large flowered hybrids through some of the roses which require less pruning. Once again if the experienced gardener requires to use a particular clematis cultivar because of the colour of the flowers, then the early flowering hybrid may be pruned harder

than generally recommended with the result that the flowering period will be delayed, the large early flowers being lost, but the desired result of colour association will be achieved. The *jackmanii* types such as 'Ascotiensis', 'Comtesse de Bouchaud', 'Gipsy Queen', 'Hagley Hybrid', 'Jackmanii Superba', 'Madame Baron Veillard', 'Madame Edouard André', 'Perle d'Azur', 'Star of India' and 'Victoria' offer various shades from blue, pink, red and purple, all of which blend well with the flowers of the shrub rose.

C. 'Ascotiensis' climbing and flowering on a wall trained rose during early August.

Propagation

The propagation of clematis is a challenging and satisfying occupation for the keen clematis grower.

There are several ways in which clematis may be reproduced, by seed, layering, cuttings, grafting and by root crown division of the herbaceous cultivars.

Reproduction by layering

The layering of clematis is not so exciting as waiting for seedlings to flower, but it is a means by which a gardener can successfully, and without much experience, increase the numbers of clematis for his own garden, or for swopping with other gardeners. The exchange of plants between gardening enthusiasts is always a satisfactory means of increasing one's own selection and a way in which plants gain wider distribution.

The best time for layering clematis is during May and June. A 10cm diameter flowerpot may be sunk into the soil near to the base of the clematis plant and within easy reach of the stem which is to be layered. The pot should contain a mixture of John Innes potting soil No. 2 and be filled to the top and lightly firmed. The selected stem may be gently bent downwards towards the pot and the nearest node to the flowerpot should be pinned into the soil with a piece of thick wire. Before the node is pinned down it may be split by a sharp knife, a 2.5cm cut made in an upward direction from below the node and into the node will help rooting to take place. When the stem is pinned onto the soil in the pot an extra layer of soil can be placed over the node and a stone may also be placed over the wire pin to hold it in place. Rooting of

Layering a clematis.

the stem may take several weeks and the soil in the flowerpot must not be allowed to become dry. After about nine months the layered stem will have formed a new plant but it should be left attached to its parent until the following March when it may be detached and the pot removed from the soil. The new plant should then be treated as if it were a plant purchased from a nursery and planted and pruned as described on pages 14 to 15.

Reproduction by seed

All clematis species may be grown successfully from seed. The resultant seedlings are generally true to type, but there may be variation, either improvements, or poorer forms than the plant from which the seed was collected. Obviously all clematis cultivars, being hybrids, cannot be reproduced true to type from seed. However, this does not put off the enthusiastic gardener who uses this disadvantage in the hope of raising a brand new clematis hybrid. Seedlings from clematis cultivars are certainly exciting because one does not know what to expect with regard to the possible colours. Seeds collected from a blue clematis may produce white, or even pink flowers. One is, therefore, left in expectation until the flower of the seedling opens with either success or disappointment. In fact, a cultivar now generally available called 'Edith', a large white clematis with red anthers was raised by me and was just a chance seedling from *Clematis* 'Mrs. Cholmondeley', a pale blue variety. Seed can be collected from the early flowering clematis in September as soon as it becomes brown, swollen and ripened. The gardener can judge when the seeds are ripened by the condition of the seed tails (styles). As the seeds ripen these seed tails become fluffy and are silky-grey in colour. The swollen seeds vary in size depending upon the variety and they are mostly dark brown in colour, breaking away from the old flower stalk when fully ripened.

Seeds of the later flowering species and cultivars do not have the opportunity to become fully ripened by September unless the weather is hot and sunny, therefore, the early flowering types are the ones to experiment with first.

Seed collected during September and October may be sown in seed trays or pots immediately after collection having removed the seed tails. Seed compost to the John Innes seed compost formula may be used and the seeds need to be covered by compost to a depth of .5cm (¼in). The container should be placed in a cold frame or glasshouse until germination takes place which may take up to six months with some cultivars. During this time the top of the container should be covered with a piece of glass and brown paper and the compost must not be allowed to dry out. As soon as germination takes place the seedlings must be given more sunlight, and as soon as they become large enough to transplant they should be potted into a 7.5cm flowerpot and grown on in a similar manner to tomatoes or other seedlings. Twelve months after germination they may be planted out into a garden position or grown on in a larger flowerpot (John Innes No. 2 potting compost) until they flower. It may take up to four years from collection of seed until the first mature flowers are produced. The waiting and patience is not always rewarded

by a brand new cultivar worthy of commercial production and sales, but I assure you, the excitement from when the first flower bud appears until the flower opens is almost too much to bear.

Reproduction by root division

This is a simple means of increasing the herbaceous clematis and may be done during January and February. An established plant may be dug up from its position and by the use of two forks placed back to back the clematis may be divided. Each piece of plant detached from the original should have roots and an old stem on which new growth buds are visible. The divided plants can then be replanted immediately and given similar treatment to a new clematis planted out from a container. It is vital to keep the divided plant's small root system moist until it becomes established.

Reproduction by cuttings

This method of propagation is for the experienced gardener and the professional nurseryman. An internodal cutting is used with the cutting taken from the soft, young stems during May, June and July from plants growing in an open garden position. Propagation from cuttings of the vigorous species is reasonably easy. The large flowered cultivars are rather more difficult. For successful rooting of cuttings a warm humid position, out of direct sunlight, is necessary.

Clematis reproduction by the use of grafting is now almost outdated and only used by some nurserymen, where cultivars are difficult to root from cuttings. The root stock of *Clematis vitalba* ("old man's beard") and *Clematis viticella* are the usual clematis used by professional growers if grafting is practised. If grafted

plants are damaged 'by mice affected by "clematis wilt" the have little chance of full recove and this is the reason why th means of reproduction has bee more or less phased out.

Pests and diseases

Fortunately clematis plants are less prone to disease or attacks by pests than many other plants, for which the clematis grower can be thankful. Like other shrubs and semi-woody plants clematis are subject to attacks from aphid, mildew and other small pests, all of which can be easily controlled without causing harm to the clematis plant. The only major problem and sometimes cause for distress is "clematis wilt". The "wilt" is possibly brought about by the presence of a fungus in a damaged part of a stem of the clematis. Unfortunately, little is known about "clematis wilt", leaving us with no definite cures or preventative measures. What previously has appeared to be a healthy plant suddenly collapses. Sometimes only a small part of a plant is affected but in some extreme cases the entire plant.

The point at which "wilt" affects the plant is generally near soil level or at least within one metre of soil level. The fungus is thought to be present in the soil previous to the attack and possibly splashed into a damaged stem which may have been twisted or cracked by wind or during cultivation. The fungus once positioned in its host grows, blocking the sap stream which causes the stem above to collapse due to lack of moisture. If such damage should occur, all affected stems and foliage must be removed immediately and burnt. After the affected stems and leaves have been removed the remaining stems can be sprayed with benlate, captan or any other sulphur-based fungicide as a possible preventative against further damage. The foliage and lower stems of the plant and surrounding soil area may be treated every four weeks until the plant ' has recovered and produced new growth, or no further collapse by "clematis wilt" is experienced. If a plant consistently "wilts" then it is best dug up, the soil removed from the root system and the plant submerged in a captan or benlate solution. The treated plant can be carefully replanted in another site, the original site should be treated again with captan or benlate, as a precaution against further attacks on plants replanted in the same position. If "clematis wilt" has become a problem in a particular garden, the preventative measures described can be used to reduce the risk of future damage.

Generally only unhealthy, old or young weak plants are affected and in most cases the clematis recovers fully within two years. New growth is produced from above or just below soil level. The important point made earlier regarding the extra depth of planting, allowing several nodes to be placed under the soil level, was intended to help the plant when damage occurs near ground level. With the extra depth of planting new growth can be almost guaranteed from below soil level even after all top growth has been removed, due to the extra dormant buds below the soil. Correct and hard pruning of clematis in the earlier years of the plant's life also help to prevent "wilt" from being fatal and assist with a quick recovery.

Slugs and snails

These delightful little beasts can be very troublesome during early spring, eating pieces out of leaves and skimming stems of young fleshy plants. The asparagus-like shoots produced by the late flowering species and cultivars are exactly what the slugs have been waiting patiently for all winter, so be warned. There are many slug baits and pellets available but a far cheaper preventative measure is to place a circle of spent coal ashes on the soil near to the main stems of the clematis, keeping the ashes at least 8-10cm from the stems. The coarseness of the ashes is unpleasant to the underparts of a slug or snail, and prevents them from crossing to where the young stems are growing.

Mice and rabbits

These slightly larger creatures also enjoy a supper or breakfast of clematis shoots and the mice also appear to like clematis stems for nesting material. Their control is therefore vital if at all possible. To prevent rabbits, a collar of very fine mesh wire netting placed around the stem to a height of one metre usually does the trick. When mice are a big problem a land drain placed over the clematis root system allows the top growth to grow through the upturned pipe which will deter mice from constant attack. When the clematis stems have become strong and woody after two years or so, the pipe, if it is unsightly, may be broken and removed because the woody stems are not so attractive to mice.

Earwigs

The plants most prone to earwig damage are those growing through a densely-foliaged evergreen, or on an old wall or outbuilding, where there are plenty of places for the earwigs to hide during daylight. The proprietary products available for their control can be used if damage is extensive. The damage is identified by holes in the foliage or a hole in the unopened flower bud. When a flower bud is the target a hole is drilled through into the cavity and in some cases the stamens are removed at differing lengths.

Glossary

- ◨ Evergreen trees (large)
- ◖◗ Evergreen trees (medium)
- ▽ Medium sized deciduous trees
- ❪❫ Large shrubs (evergreen)
- ❪❫ Large shrubs (deciduous)
- ▦ Ground cover
- ◣ Very low shrubs
- ▦ Coverage large wall areas
- ▰ Wall trained shrubs
- ∩ Pergolas and archways

NAME	PRINCIPAL COLOUR	SIZE AND SHAPE OF FLOWER	HEIGHT	FACING POSITION
alpina 'Columbine'	Pale blue	Small nodding	2.5-3m	Any
alpina 'Pamela Jackman'	Mid blue	Small nodding	2.5-3m	Any
alpina 'Ruby'	Purple pink	Small nodding	2.5-3m	Any
alpina 'White Moth'	White	Small nodding	2.5m	Any
armandii	White	Small	3m	Sheltered site
'Ascotiensis'	Bright blue	Large	3m	Any
'Barbara Dibley'	Petunia red	Large	2.5-3m	South, west, east
'Barbara Jackman'	Blue, petunia bar	Large	2.5-3m	North, east, west
'Beauty of Richmond'	Pale lavender	Large	3m	Any
'Beauty of Worcester'	Pale lavender	Large	3m	Any
'Bees Jubilee'	Deep pink, rose bar	Large	2.5m	North, east, west
'Bracebridge Star'	Lavender, carmine bar	Large	2.5-3m	North, east, west
chrysocoma	Soft pink	Small	6m	Any
cirrhosa (calycina)	Creamy yellow	Small nodding	3m	Sheltered south
cirrhosa balearica	Creamy yellow	Small nodding	3m	Sheltered south
'Comtesse de Bouchaud'	Mauve pink	Large	4m	Any
'Corona'	Light purple pink	Large	2.5m	Any
'Countess of Lovelace'	Pale lilac blue	Large, double and semi-double	2.5-3m	South, west, east
'Daniel Deronda'	Purple blue	Large, double and semi-double	3m	South, west, east
'Dawn'	Pearly white	Large	2.5m	West, east
'Duchess of Edinburgh'	White	Medium double	2.5m	South, west, east
'Duchess of Sutherland'	Carmine	Large	3m	Any
x *durandii* (syn.*semperflorens*)	Indigo blue	Medium	2.5m	Any
'Edith'	White	Large	3m	Any
'Elsa Späth'	Mid blue	Large	3m	Any
x *eriostemon* 'Hendersonii'	Indigo blue	Small	2.5m	Any
'Ernest Markham'	Magenta	Large	3.5m	South, west, east
'Fair Rosamund'	White, pink bar	Large	2m	West, east
'Fairy Queen'	Flesh, rose bar	Large	3m	North, west, east
fargesii var. *souliei*	White	Small	4-5m	Any
flammula	White	Small, star shaped	4-5m	Any
florida bicolor (syn. 'Sieboldii')	White, purple centre	Medium	2.5m	Sheltered south, west
'Gipsy Queen'	Violet purple	Large	4m	Any
'Hagley Hybrid'	Rosy mauve	Medium	2.5m	North, west, east
'Henryi'	Creamy white	Large	3m	Any
heracleifolia 'Davidiana'	Pale blue	Small clusters	75cm	Any
heracleifolia 'Wyevale'	Mid blue	Small clusters	75cm	Any
'H. F. Young'	Wedgwood blue	Large	2.5m	Any
'Horn of Plenty'	Deep rosy mauve	Large	2.5m	Any
'Huldine'	Pearly white	Medium	5m	Any
integrifolia	Indigo blue	Small nodding	70cm	Any
integrifolia 'Hendersonii'	Indigo blue	Small nodding	75cm	Any
'Jackmanii Alba'	Off white	Large double and semi-double	2.5m	Any
'Jackmanii Superba'	Dark purple	Large	3m	Any
'John Warren'	Dark pink	Large	3m	North, west, east
x *jouiniana* 'Praecox'	Pale lavender	Small clusters	2.5m	Any
'Kathleen Wheeler'	Plummy mauve	Large	3m	Any
'King Edward VII'	Puce violet, crimson bar	Large	2.5m	North, west, east
'Lady Betty Balfour'	Purple	Large	3.5m	South, west, east
'Lady Caroline Nevill'	Blue mauve	Large, semi-double	3m	South, west, east
'Lady Londesborough'	Pale mauve blue	Medium	2m	South, west, east
'Lady Northcliffe'	Wedgwood blue	Medium	2m	Any
'Lasurstern'	Blue	Large	3m	Any

Legend:
- Shrub roses
- Container culture
- Suitable for cut flowers
- Attractive seed heads

FLOWER SIZE.

Small = up to 5 cm diameter

Medium = 5 cm to 10 cm diameter

Large = larger than 10 cm diameter

PRUNING CODE

GROUP ONE	= TIDY AFTER FLOWERING
GROUP TWO	= LIGHT FEB-MARCH
GROUP THREE	= HARD FEB-MARCH

FLOWERING MONTHS	PRUNING CODE	OUTSTANDING FEATURES	MOST SUITABLE POSITION OR HOSTS
April	1.	Very hardy, ideal for a north wall	
April	1.	Hardy, attractive seed heads	
April-May	1.	Occasional flowers in summer months	
April	1.	Attractive double flowers	
March-April	1.	Large evergreen foliage, slightly scented flowers	
July-Sept.	3.	Delightful with red roses	
May, June and Aug.	2.	Red anthers	
May, June and Aug.	2.	Yellow anthers	
June-Aug.	2.	Very large flowers	
June-Aug.	2.	Cream anthers, fully double and single flowers	
May, June and Aug.	2.	Light brown anthers free flowering	
May-June	2.	Red anthers	
May	1.	Attractive downy foliage	
Jan.-March	1.	Delightful evergreen foliage, semi-hardy	
Jan.-March	1.	Finely cut evergreen foliage, semi-hardy	
July-Aug.	3.	Very free flowering	
May, June and Aug.	2.	Red anthers, compact plant	
May, June and Aug.	2.	Double flowers on old stems followed by single flowers	
May, June and Aug.	2.	Yellow anthers, double, semi-double and single flowers	
May-June	2.	Red anthers, compact plant	
June-Aug.	2.	Fully double flowers	
June-Aug.	2.	Creamy yellow anthers	
July-Aug.	3.	Creamy anthers, thick sepals, semi-herbaceous	
May, June-Aug, Sept.	2.	Red anthers, free flowering	
May-Sept.	2.	Red anthers, strong free flowering	
July-Sept.	3.	First hybrid clematis raised, non-clinging habit	
July-end Sept.	3.	Light brown anthers, outstanding "red" clematis	
May-June	2.	Red anthers, slightly scented	
June-Aug.	2.	Very large flowers	
Late June-Sept.	3.	Strong free flowering	
Aug.-Oct.	3.	Thousands of tiny scented flowers	
Late June-Sept.	3.	Delightful flowers, sometimes mistaken for a passion flower	
July-Aug.	3.	Dark, red anthers	
Late June-Aug.	3.	Red anthers, compact plant, free flowering	
June-Aug.	2.	Brown anthers, old established cultivar	
Aug.-Sept.	3.	Hyacinth-like flowers, herbaceous habit, scented	Herbaceous plant
Aug.-Sept.	3.	Similar to foregoing cultivar, darker flowers	Herbaceous plant
May, June and Aug.	2.	Creamy anther, compact habit free flowering	
May, June and Aug.	2.	Red anthers, very large attractive flowers	
July-Sept.	3.	Free flowering, vigorous habit	
July	3.	Compact herbaceous habit	Herbaceous plant
July	3.	Large form of the foregoing	Herbaceous plant
June-Aug.	2.	Double on old wood, single new growth	
July-Aug.	3.	Free flowering, the most popular clematis	
May, June and Aug.	2.	Red anthers, free flowering, very large flowers	
July-Sept.	3.	Non-clinging, vigorous plant	
June-Sept.	2.	Yellow anthers, very large flowers	
June-Aug.	2.	Light brown anthers	
Late Aug.-Oct.	3.	Yellow anthers, late flowering	
June-Aug.	2.	Semi-double flowers on old wood, single new growth	
May-June	2.	Red anthers, very early flowering, compact plant	
June-Aug.	2.	Yellow anthers, compact plant	
May-June and Aug.-Sept.	2.	Creamy yellow anthers, very handsome flowers	

73

NAME	PRINCIPAL COLOUR	SIZE AND SHAPE OF FLOWER	HEIGHT	FACING POSITION
'Lincoln Star'	Raspberry pink	Large	2.5m	North, west, east
'Lord Nevill'	Dark blue	Large	3m	Any
macropetala	Blue	Small nodding	2.5m	Any
macropetala 'Markhams Pink'	Pink	Small nodding	2.5m	Any
'Madame Baron Veillard'	Lilac rose	Medium	3.5m	South, west, east
'Madame Edouard André'	Dusky red	Medium	3m	Any
'Marie Boisselot' (syn. 'Madame le Coultre')	White	Large	3.5m	Any
'Maureen'	Purple	Large	3m	Any
maximowicziana (syn. paniculata)	White	Small star shaped	6m	Sunny, sheltered
'Miss Bateman'	Creamy white	Medium	2m	South, west, east
montana	Snow white	Small	9m	Any
montana 'Elizabeth'	Soft pink	Small	8m	Any
montana 'Picton's Variety'	Deep satin pink	Small	5m	Any
montana rubens	Pale mauve pink	Small	8.5m	Any
montana 'Tetrarose'	Deep rosy mauve	Medium	5m	Any
'Mrs. Bush'	Deep lavender	Large	3m	Any
'Mrs. Cholmondeley'	Light blue	Large	3m	Any
'Mrs. George Jackman'	Creamy white	Large semi-double	2.5m	Any
'Mrs. N. Thompson'	Blue petunia bar	Large	2.5m	North, west, east
'Mrs. P. B. Truax'	Periwinkle blue	Medium	2m	South, west, east
'Nelly Moser'	Mauve lilac bar	Large	2.5m	North, west, east
'Niobe'	Velvety red	Large	3m	Any
orientalis 'Burford Variety'	Deep yellow	Small nodding	5m	Any
orientalis 'L & S 13342'	Yellow	Small nodding	4.5m	Any
'Perle d'Azur'	Azure	Medium	3.5m	Any
'Proteus'	Mauve pink	Large double	3m	West, south, east
recta	White	Small (very tiny)	1.75m	Any
'Richard Pennell'	Very deep lavender	Large	3m	Any
'Rouge Cardinale'	Rich magenta	Large	2.5-3m	Any
'Serenata'	Dusky purple	Large	3.5m	Any
serratifolia	Pale yellow	Small nodding	6m	Any
'Sir Garnet Wolseley'	Mauve blue	Medium	3m	Any
'Star of India'	Deep purple, carmine bar	Medium	3.5m	Any
tangutica	Yellow	Small nodding	5m	Any
texensis 'Duchess of Albany'	Deep pink	Small tulip like	2m	Any
texensis 'Gravetye Beauty'	Ruby red	Small tulip like	2m	Any
'The President'	Rich purple	Large	3m	Any
vedrariensis 'Highdown'	Pink	Small	6m	Any
'Victoria'	Rosy purple	Medium	3.5m	Any
'Ville de Lyon'	Carmine red	Large	3m	West, east
vitalba	Creamy white	Small star like	8m	Any
viticella 'Abundance'	Rosy red	Small semi-nodding	3.5m	Any
viticella 'Alba Luxurians'	Creamy white	Small semi-nodding	3.5m	Any
viticella 'Etoile Violette'	Violet	Medium	4m	Any
viticella 'Little Nell'	White mauve	Small	3.5m	Any
viticella 'Madame Julia Correvon'	Wine red	Small semi-nodding	3.5m	Any
viticella 'Margot Koster'	Deep pink-mauve	Small semi-campanulate	3.5m	Any
viticella 'Minuet'	White mauve	Small semi-campanulate	3.5m	Any
viticella 'Purpurea Plena Elegans'	Purple-mauve	Small double	3.5m	Any
viticella 'Royal Velours'	Deep purple	Medium	3.5m	Any
viticella 'Rubra'	Wine red	Small	3.5m	Any
viticella 'Venosa Violacea'	White and purple	Medium	3.5m	Any
'Vyvyan Pennell'	Lavender	Large double and single	3m	South, west, east
'W. E. Gladstone'	Pale blue	Large	4m	Any
'William Kennett'	Pale blue	Large	3.5m	Any
'Yellow Queen'	Primrose yellow	Large	3m	West, east

FLOWERING MONTHS	PRUNING CODE	OUTSTANDING FEATURES
May-June and Aug.	2.	Red anthers, August flowers paler colouring
June-Aug.	2.	Red anthers, attractive flower
April-May	1.	Free flowering, hardy plant, attractive seed heads
April-May	1.	Delightful pink form of the foregoing
Sept.-Oct.	3.	Very late flowering
Late June-Aug.	3.	Yellow anthers, free flowering
June-end Sept.	2.	Best white clematis, good foliage
June-Aug.	2.	Light brown anthers, beautiful flowers
Sept.-beg. Oct.	3.	Vigorous, scented, needs hot summer to flower well
May-June	2.	Red anthers, compact plant
May-June	1.	Rampant vigorous plant
May-June	1.	Fragrant flowers
May-June	1.	Occasional summer flowers
May-June	1.	Pink form of montana
May-June	1.	Attractive foliage
June-Aug.	2.	Light chocolate anthers, very large flowers
May-Sept.	2.	Very free flowering
May-June and Aug.	2.	Semi-double old wood, single flowers new growth
May-June and Aug.	2.	Red anthers, pretty flowers
May-June	2.	Yellow anthers, compact plant
May-June, Aug.-Sept.	2.	Red anthers, dinstinctive flowers
June-Sept.	2.	Yellow anthers, superb colours
July-Oct.	3.	Vigorous free flowering, attractive seed heads
July-Oct.	3.	Thick sepals, attractive foliage
July-Sept.	3.	Very attractive, semi-campanulate flowers
May-June and Aug.	2.	Fully double, semi-double and single flowers
July	3.	Vigorous, scented, herbaceous variety

Herbaceous plant

May-June and Aug.	2.	Creamy yellow anthers, outstanding colours
June-Sept.	2.	Free flowering over a long period
June-Sept.	2.	Yellow anthers, very deep coloured sepals
July-Oct.	3.	Dark red anthers, rampant plant
May-June	2.	Red anthers, compact free flowering
July-end Aug.	3	Free flowering
Aug.-Sept.	3.	Masses of flowers followed by seed heads
July-Sept.	3.	Delightfully shaped flowers
July-Sept.	3.	Gorgeous coloured flowers
May-Sept.	2.	Good, reliable, free flowering
May-June	1.	Free flowering montana type, downy foliage
July-Aug.	3.	Free flowering
Late June-Sept.	3.	Yellow anthers, good flowers, untidy foliage
July-Sept.	3.	Thousands of flowers, and attractive seed heads
July-Sept.	3.	Very free flowering
July-Sept.	3.	Delightful twisted sepals
July-Sept.	3.	Prominent creamy yellow anthers
July-Sept.	3.	Dainty flowers
Late June-Sept.	3.	Creamy yellow anthers, recurving sepals
July-Sept.	3.	Free flowering gappy flowers
July-Sept.	3.	Most attractive colouring
July-Sept.	3.	Superb free flowering double cultivar
July-Sept.	3.	Black anthers, very deep colouring
July-Sept.	3.	Black anthers
July-Sept.	3.	Boat shaped sepals, most unusual
May-June and Aug.	2.	Best double clematis, single on new growth
June-Aug.	2.	Red anthers, the largest flowered cultivar
June-Aug.	2.	Red anthers, sepals have crimpled edges
May-June	2.	Yellow anthers, interesting foliage

MOST SUITABLE POSITION OR HOSTS

Index

Note: figures in bold denote illustrations